Up All Night

Up All Night

Graham Masterton

A SIGNET BOOK

SIGNET
Published by New American Library, a division of
Penguin Group (USA) Inc., 375 Hudson Street,
New York, New York 10014, U.S.A.
Penguin Books Ltd, 80 Strand,
London WC2R 0RL, England
Penguin Books Australia Ltd, 250 Camberwell Road,
Camberwell, Victoria 3124, Australia
Penguin Books Canada Ltd, 10 Alcorn Avenue,
Toronto, Ontario, Canada M4V 3B2
Penguin Books (N.Z.) Ltd, Cnr Rosedale and Airborne Roads,
Albany, Auckland 1310, New Zealand

Penguin Books Ltd, Registered Offices:
80 Strand, London WC2R 0RL, England

First published by Signet, an imprint of New American Library,
a division of Penguin Group (USA) Inc.

First Printing, March 2004
10 9 8 7 6 5 4 3 2 1

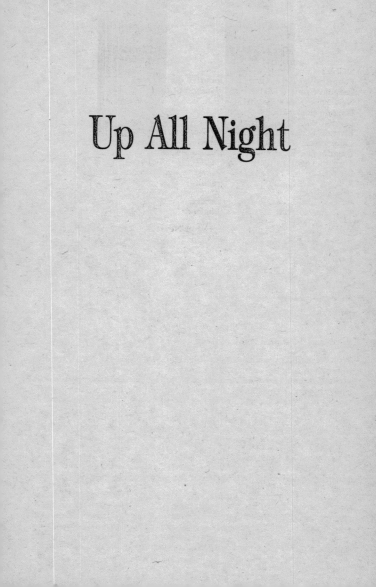

Up All Night

Foreword

Up, Up and Away

Question: What is the number-one essential for a great sexual relationship?

Passion? No, not passion, even though passion's good. Not romance, either, although a sexual relationship without romance is like a good meal without wine. Neither is it friendship, nor laughter, nor a mutual interest in country-and-western, say—or baseball or Italian cooking, although all of these things are a bonus.

You and your partner can have a great sexual relationship regardless of your age, your race, your education or your upbringing. If you share a taste for sexual specialties—spanking or bondage or making love in the great outdoors—then you can have some truly wild times together. But again, these are not absolute necessities.

It might seem blatantly obvious, but the number-one essential is a penis that goes up—and not only goes up, but stays up.

Anyone who has read any of my previous books

on sexual pleasure will know that you don't necessarily have to have intercourse to enjoy a really incredible time in bed. But although there are hundreds of ways to have fun without the man in your life having a full or a lasting erection, there is no way that you can pretend that any long-term sexual relationship is 100 percent fulfilling without it. Let's put it like this: it's fun to sit in a Cadillac. You can play with the steering wheel and the six-way seats and the CD player. But if the engine won't fire up—or the engine fires up but keeps dying away after only a few yards of driving—you'll soon start to feel extremely shortchanged. Resentful, even. And it's the same with your sex life. **Erectile dysfunction**—or **ED**, as it's commonly called—is the principal cause of sexual unhappiness bar none. And much more than sexual unhappiness: it can have a corrosive effect on every aspect of your relationship.

This book is all about getting your man erect and keeping him erect, so that you can both enjoy the best sex you ever had—and for longer. It's not written exclusively for women whose partners have serious and persistent difficulty in getting it up (although I will be showing you how you can work miracles with even the most hopeless cases of floppy-itis). It's also written for women whose partners are ordinary everyday guys who don't usually have very much trouble in getting a boner. You see, ordinary everyday guys tend to take their potency for granted, and don't realize how much their erections could be improved and prolonged by exercise, diet, and mental self-discipline, not to mention all kinds of other tricks. Just because they can achieve an erection without any trouble, they don't appreciate that they could get it up very much harder and for very much longer. They should also be thinking about the years that lie ahead, when general unfitness can take a very serious toll on a man's virility.

Your love life could be ten times more exciting if you knew how to get the best out of your partner's penis. Do you think your man is good enough in bed? How good is good enough? Is he hard enough, big enough, and does he keep going long enough? With the knowledge you acquire in this book, you will be able to turn your lover into an all-night superstud. Not only that, you will have far greater control over *when* you make love and *how* you make love and how long it lasts. If you can make your partner's penis do things that even *he* can't make it do, then guess who's going to have the upper hand in bed?

In this book I will be telling you clearly how a man's erection works, so that you can make him stiff and keep him stiffer for longer, and so that you *both* get much more satisfaction out of your sex life.

I will explain *why* a man gets an erection, and just as importantly, why he doesn't. I will discuss the truth about penis size and penis enlargement. Is a penis really so much better if it's bigger—and if it is, can you *really* add on inches? And how? With exercise? With pills? And what about surgery?

Most importantly, I will let you into a startling

new secret which gives you the power to convince your partner that his penis is more than big enough . . . even if he's worried that it isn't.

I will discuss techniques for keeping your man's penis erect all night . . . and how to stir it back into life when even *he* thought he could never get it up again. I will tell you how you can tire him out so much that he never wants to *think* about having sex with another woman.

I will also be totally frank about what *doesn't* work, when it comes to getting and keeping an erection. There are so many phony pills and treatments and exercise plans on the market, some of them very expensive—and none of them will help your man to be longer or harder or more of a stallion. I will show you how to avoid wasting your time and your money, and how to avoid the bitter frustration that always follows when a so-called "erection treatment" proves to be useless.

Men with erection problems are always fair game for hucksters, because no man likes to admit that he can't get it up—even if it only happens now and again. Most men are very reluctant to talk to anybody about it, even their closest friends. They don't feel like "real men," and the effect on their sexual relationships and their day-to-day lives can be catastrophic.

At the same time, many women fail to understand that most men suffer some erectile dysfunction at some period in their lives, for one reason or another. But their inability to get a hard-on is *very rarely* caused by a loss of interest in sex, or because they no longer find their partner sexually attractive.

In the majority of cases, men with erection difficulties are absolutely *desperate* to make love. The only reason they start to act cold and withdrawn is because they can't bear to go through the frustration and humiliation of trying to achieve an erection and not being able to manage it. As one man told me, "There's only one way to describe it—it's totally demeaning. That's why I stopped trying. It was less humiliating to pretend that I wasn't interested, rather than admit that I simply couldn't get it up."

In the past few years, however, there has been far more open discussion about erection problems, in magazines and newspapers and on the Internet. At the same time, the arrival of genuinely helpful drugs such as Viagra and Cialis has dramatically changed the lives of countless men who thought that their sex lives were effectively over. Dedicated medical experts have done some truly brilliant work to demystify the subject, financially supported by the pharmaceutical industry.

Provided he is prepared to seek help, there is no longer any need for any man who is worried about his virility to think that he is doomed to spend the rest of his life in celibate misery.

Jack, 33, a computer technician from Milwaukee, Wisconsin, told me that his failure to sustain an erection almost ended his marriage. "I was working for a large computer-maintenance company, but I didn't get along with my boss and I decided it was time to strike out on my own. I borrowed money from the bank and set up my own business, specializing in home visits to fix people's computers.

"Up until then, our marriage had been fine, I mean the sex side of it. We made love three or four times a week and it was always good. Ellie had this special fantasy about being taken by force, if you know what I mean, like the women in those historical fiction stories. She liked it if I pinned her down on the bed and pulled off her panties and did it kind of rough.

"But then my business ran into trouble. Cash flow, mainly. I lost a couple of guys because I couldn't afford to pay them. Then I had to borrow more money from the bank, and things started to go downhill. I felt like I couldn't take care of my family and I began to get these bouts of depression. Being in debt, that doesn't do a lot for your manhood, let me tell you. I found it difficult to keep my erections all the way through our lovemaking, so I went to the doctor about my depression and he prescribed some pills.

"Instead of getting better, though, my performance in bed started to get even worse. Ellie still wanted to be ravished but you try ravishing a woman with a soft cock. It's just impossible, and you end up feeling, like, totally inadequate. I think that's what upset me the most . . . the futility of trying to push this squishy little thing into a woman who was panting for a big, hard erection. It would have been funny if it hadn't been so sad.

"The more I tried, the worse it got. The usual pattern was, I got an erection, I got on top of her as quickly as I could before it died away, but then it died away anyhow. Ellie told me not to worry but I could tell that she was just as worried as I was, and confused, too. I did my best to satisfy her using my tongue and my fingers. I managed to give her orgasms, for sure, but it wasn't the same as fucking her. I used to lie awake in bed after she had gone to sleep and I felt so miserable and useless that I used to cry. I felt like a eunuch.

"Ellie didn't seem to understand that a man's cock has a mind of its own. It's not the Indian rope trick: if it doesn't feel like going up, it won't. So the trouble is, when I couldn't get a hard-on, she started to take it personally, like I was doing it on purpose to make her feel unattractive, or to show her how tired and hardworking I was. She used to rub my cock up and down fast and furious like she was pumping up a bicycle tire, trying to make it hard, and she simply couldn't understand why it wouldn't go stiff. First of all she blamed herself, and thought that she wasn't holding it right. Then she accused me of deliberately staying soft because I didn't feel like making love to her. As if! We argued all the time, and in the end we stopped even trying to have sex. I think that if she had found another man at that time, our marriage would have been over."

Fortunately for Jack—at his wits' end—he confided in his father. "To my surprise, Dad said that *he* was having sexual problems, too. I mean, you don't even think of your parents still having sex, do you? But he used to be a real heavy smoker when he was younger, twenty or thirty a day, and apparently a lot of heavy smokers have trouble getting erections when they grow older. He sent me along to his own specialist, and the first thing this doctor did was to ask me why I thought I couldn't get an erection. I told him I was depressed and worried about money, and he said, sure, that's right, depression can seriously affect your potency. But then he asked me if I was taking any antidepressants.

"When I told him that I was on Nortryptyline, he said immediately—that's it. There's your problem. The tablets were lifting my depression but they were affecting my potency. I stopped taking them, and within two or three days I was almost back to normal. I was able to go back to Ellie and say, this is why I couldn't get it up. Nothing to do with not loving you. My depression caused the problem in the first place but the cure for my depression made it worse.

"The first time that Ellie and I made love, I was terrified that I was going to lose my erection, and halfway through I began to feel my cock going soft inside her. But then I did like the specialist had told me, and relaxed, and took a deep mental breath, and before I knew it I was fully hard again.

"I still worry about the business, and we haven't yet turned the corner financially, but the most important thing in my life is that I know that I'm physically a man. I can take my wife out and put my arm around her and look everybody in the eye—which, believe me, is something I couldn't do when I couldn't get a hard-on, because it made me feel like a fraud. I don't care how it sounds: if you can look at your wife when she's all dressed up and talking to her friends and you can think to yourself, I fucked you last night, you beautiful lady—that means something, and any man who says it doesn't is a liar."

Jack's original difficulty in keeping an erection was caused by what we call **psychogenic impotence**—that is, impotence which can be traced to psychological problems such as stress and anxiety, or perhaps by separation or bereavement or some other traumatic event. In Jack's case, of course, it was worry about money.

Of all the young men under 35 who seek help from their doctors for erection trouble, over 70 percent of them are suffering from purely psychogenic impotence, and not from any physical ailment.

In this book I'll be taking a look at some of the most frequent causes of psychogenic impotence—how to recognize them and what you can do to sort them out. Even if your lover is reluctant to go for professional counseling, I'll show you how your help and your understanding can simultaneously lift his spirits (and his penis).

One of the biggest problems with psychogenic impotence is that—having failed to achieve an erection on two or three occasions—a man develops a recurring "fear of failure" which affects him every time he tries to make love. "Will I be able to keep it up this time?" he asks himself, in the back of his mind, and the minute he does so, his erection begins to die away. The more he concentrates on getting it back again, the less likely he is to do so. As Jack so accurately describes it, penises have minds of their own.

Jack was also suffering from **pharmacological impotence**. This simply means that his ability to achieve an erection was affected by the drugs he was taking. Men who rely on antidepressants or pills to control their blood pressure often have trouble getting erections (although it's important that they don't stop taking any prescribed medicine until they have discussed it with their doctors).

Apart from impotence caused by mental problems and by drugs, there is also **organic impotence**. This is most commonly caused by narrowing of the arteries—atherosclerosis—which is brought on by the one thing that even the greatest stud in the world can never avoid—growing older.

Narrow arteries restrict the flow of blood into your partner's penis . . . and it's the flow of blood into the penis which makes it go hard. Atherosclerosis is also aggravated by smoking. Like Jack's father, many comparatively young smokers find that their twenty-a-day habit has affected their sexual performance, and that they have the erection difficulties of men who are ten years older than they are.

There are several other organic causes of erectile dysfunction, such as heart disease, diabetes and neurological problems, which we can look at later. But even in very serious cases, you can always do something positive to improve your sexual enjoyment.

Maybe the man in your life has absolutely no trouble at all in achieving and keeping an erection, but there are still scores of ways in which you can improve his staying power. Some of these techniques go way back into antiquity, and were developed by the courtesans of ancient China and the houris of India. Others have been discovered by modern sexual research, especially that of Masters and Johnson, whose clinical work on premature ejaculation (climaxing too soon) was revolutionary.

But the key element in keeping your man's penis up all night is *you*—the way in which you think about his sexual equipment and the confidence with which you handle it. Don't tell the man in your life: the secret of achieving a really hard and lasting erection is *yours*.

Their results may not have been very politically correct, but recent studies into male and female behavior have reinforced the anecdotal evidence that men tend to be more mechanical and practical in their view of life and women tend to be more intuitive and emotional. When a man's penis is reluctant to work, his first reaction is that it's a technical problem. He will put it down to too much booze, too little sleep, too much stress at work.

Women, on the other hand, tend to regard sex much more emotionally, and if a man has difficulty in performing, a woman's first suspicion, like Jack's wife Ellie, is that "he doesn't find me attractive any more."

There is no doubt that your partner's potency can be seriously affected if you're going through a bad patch, or you're right on the verge of splitting up. People fall in and out of love, and no amount of Viagra is ever going to change that. But I am assuming for the purpose of this book that your relationship is in pretty reasonable shape with the exception of your lover's stiffie . . . either it's not getting stiff and staying stiff, or else you'd like it stiffer more frequently, and for longer.

If you teach yourself how his erection works and how to fix it when it doesn't—in other words, if you become a competent sex mechanic—you will be more help to your lover than a dozen doctors.

- Learn how his penis functions. Even if he doesn't have any erection problems, you can make it stiffen more quickly and stay harder longer.
- If he *does* have erection problems, learn how to find out what's causing them . . . even if he's reluctant to tell you.
- Learn his secret anxieties about his erection failure, and how to conquer them. Even if he won't admit what's going on in his head, you can help him to handle those negative thoughts that cause him to lose his hard-on right in the middle of making love.
- Above all, stop worrying that he doesn't love you, or that you don't turn him on anymore. Your positive attitude will help *him* to feel positive, too. And remember—the quicker you act to sort out your lover's erection problems, the easier they will be to overcome.

Sylvia, 28, a flight attendant from Tampa, Florida, married Barry within five weeks of meeting him on a trip to Mexico City. She had been in two long-term sexual relationships before . . . in fact, she had just finished a tempestuous three-year affair with a musician called Paul, who had treated her very abusively.

She had some practical experience of manipulating a man's genitals, although she was fairly vague about what happened when she did. "I wouldn't know how a man's cock gets hard. Is it a muscular thing? I guess we learned about sex at school but I can't really remember all of the physical details.

"I used to enjoy sex with Neal, who was the boyfriend I was living with before Paul. He was much more gentle and relaxed, you know, and some evenings we used to lie on a blanket naked with candles all around us and listen to music and just fondle each other. I hadn't really looked at a man's cock and balls before Neal, not studied them close-up, because you don't, really, do you, when you're making love? You're much more, like, looking into his eyes, and most of the time I keep my eyes closed, anyhow, especially when I'm coming close to my climax.

"Before Neal I guess I used to think that a man's cock was kind of mysterious and yucky. My mom was very prudish about sex. When I was a girl we saw some guys running around naked on the beach and she was totally, like, *shudder-shudder-shudder*! The first couple of guys I had sex with, at high school, I hardly even saw their cocks properly, although one of them, Bobby, was always trying to get me to suck him.

"The first guy I ever gave oral sex to properly was Neal, because it just happened naturally. We were lying in bed one morning and I started to fondle his cock. Then I kissed it and licked it, and I was amazed

how quickly it went hard. I loved it. I went on sucking him and kissing him until he came all over my
face and my hair and my fingers, everywhere. I had
never actually seen actual sperm before. It gave me
a real sense of achievement that *I* had done something to satisfy *him*, do you understand what I mean?
It also gave me a sense of being in control, because
I could turn him on whenever I felt like it and I
could make it last as long as I wanted to.

"I gave Neal oral sex two or three times a week,
maybe. When I told my best friend about it, she was
like, how can you let a guy humiliate you like that?
But there was never anything humiliating about it.
The opposite, really, because if I didn't *feel* like giving
him oral sex, there was no way that I had to do it. I
guess I learned that if I wanted a man to get an
instant hard-on, that was a real good technique. I
also learned how to rub his cock with my hand at
the same time as sucking it, to make him come
quicker. After my experience with Neal, men's cocks
weren't so mysterious any more."

Maybe they weren't so *physically* mysterious, but
when her new husband Barry began to suffer erection problems shortly after marrying Sylvia, she
began to worry that she had made a terrible mistake,
and that Barry didn't love her at all.

"The first time it happened was after we had been
to a party at Barry's office. He works for this realty-
development company that buys up land all the way
around the Gulf and builds vacation property on it.
It's a pretty high-pressure job but he makes a whole
lot of money. Anyhow, it was a great party and I got

lots of compliments and when we came home I was really in the mood for making love. I did a very erotic striptease and then I took off Barry's clothes. He's a great-looking guy. His hair's thinning on top but he's got a terrific body with a hairy chest. Very masculine, you know.

"The trouble was, he couldn't get his cock up. He climbed on top of me and tried to get it in, but it was much too soft. He began to get angry with it, like he was shouting at somebody at work. You know, like, 'What the hell's the matter with you, cock! Get hard or else!' I rolled him over and I sucked it for him, and he managed half a hard-on, but as soon as he tried to get it into me, it went all soft again.

"He said that he had drunk too much at the party, and that we'd try again in the morning, when he was sober. As a matter of fact, he woke me up in the middle of the night and tried it again, and he almost made it, but then it went soft again and he had to give up. He was so furious I couldn't believe it."

Barry did manage to achieve an erection in the morning, and keep it long enough to reach a climax. But when he tried to make love to Sylvia the following evening, his penis refused to rise at all. He blamed it on tiredness, and the fact that he had been drinking with his colleagues after work to celebrate the closure of a new deal. Sylvia wasn't particularly disturbed, because she didn't necessarily expect to have sex every single day. But when it came to the weekend, he was still unable to manage an erection.

"That weekend was miserable. I could tell Barry

was worried, but he wouldn't talk about it and I didn't know how to bring the subject up without making him feel worse. What was I going to do, sit there over lunch and say, 'By the way, you know how you haven't been able to get a hard-on? Well, you know, it's fine by me.' It's a very difficult thing to discuss, right? and it *wasn't* fine by me. I was already beginning to think that maybe Barry didn't find me as exciting as he did before we were married. Maybe he was feeling trapped, and we shouldn't have married at all. You have no idea the things that go through your head.

"On Sunday afternoon I tried to act all sexy and loving and while he was sitting on the couch watching TV I started kissing him and running my fingers through his hair and then I pulled down his zipper and slid my hand into his pants. I massaged his cock for a while but absolutely nothing happened. In the end he said, 'I'm not really in the mood, honey . . . I just want to watch the game.' So I took my hand out of his pants and that was that.

"I felt so useless. I felt like I couldn't even turn on my husband. When we went to bed that night he kissed me and turned over and didn't make any attempt to make love to me.

"Things went from bad to worse. Every day that week he came home late from the office smelling of drink, and every night he went to sleep without trying to have sex. He tried again on Saturday morning and he managed an erection that was just about hard enough to get inside me, but it didn't last more than a couple of minutes. In the end he gave up and got out of bed and he was in a bad mood for the rest of the weekend."

Eventually, Sylvia managed to pluck up the courage to discuss Barry's erection problem. He tried to make light of it, saying that he was going through a difficult period at work, and that everything would be fine once his latest development had been completed. He swore to Sylvia that he still loved her and found her attractive, and blamed alcohol for his inability to perform in bed. But he claimed that going to bars with his clients was part and parcel of his job, and if he didn't drink, they would consider him antisocial.

When Sylvia talked to Barry's colleagues, however, she found that no business meetings were taking place in bars, and that Barry was always the one who would suggest they went for drinks after office hours. If nobody wanted to join him, he would often go off to drink on his own.

Barry was a typical victim of "fear of failure." Having once found himself unable to achieve an erection because he had drunk too much alcohol, he was then worried that he might not be able to achieve an erection the next time. But his worry itself was self-fulfilling, because it caused his erection to die away in midintercourse, and so made matters worse. The next time, he couldn't get an erection at all.

It was at this point that Barry and Sylvia needed to work together to reestablish Barry's sexual confidence. That is why I always stress that erection problems need to be faced up to as soon as they happen, and dealt with quickly, before "fear of failure" takes a hold. Without immediate recognition that something needs to be done, erection problems can lead to feelings of depression and inadequacy on the part of the man, while women grow increasingly baffled, frustrated and resentful. If you don't talk about ED, it doesn't sort itself out on its own. It invariably gets worse, and the longer you leave it, the more difficult it is to overcome.

Barry drank for two reasons: to blur his anxiety that he wasn't a real man any more, and to have an external cause that he could blame for his lack of sexual performance (the booze). But Sylvia was able to help him over his problems in less than three weeks, simply by recognizing that he was trapped by his own fear.

On my advice, her first move was to start making sexual advances to him very early in the morning— sometimes when he was still asleep. At seven a.m., the droop-inducing effects of last night's drinking had worn off, and like most healthy men, Barry experienced a natural erection as he woke—the so-called morning glory. He was also less psychologically defensive at that time of the morning. He hadn't been fretting about his erection difficulties all day, and worrying how he was going to avoid the humiliation of trying to make love, and failing.

"I woke him up by gently sucking his cock. I didn't rush him, and I tried not to give him the feeling that I expected anything from him. When he got hard, I drew down the sheets and knelt between his legs, so that he could watch me sucking him. I made a real performance of it, closing my eyes and going *'Mmmmmm,'* as if his cock was just about the most delicious thing ever. I licked him all around his balls, too, and rubbed him with my hand. Then I turned around so that my pussy was right in front of his face while I sucked him."

Sylvia made no attempt to initiate intercourse, and on the first three occasions she tried this sexual reveille, she sucked Barry all the way to a climax. When he ejaculated, she made sure that she gave him an erotic visual spectacle that would stick in his mind. On the first occasion she let his sperm drip slowly from her lower lip and onto his stomach. The next time she massaged it sensually around her breasts. She did this for the same reason that she turned around into the "69" position while sucking his penis, so that he was looking directly at her wide-open vulva—to take his mind off himself and his erection problem.

Men who are anxious about achieving and keeping their erections tend to detach themselves mentally during lovemaking and observe their performance as if they are spectators. "Spectatoring" has the effect of insulating a man from his spontaneous sexual responses, and causes his erection to subside. Some men who *don't* have erection problems use "spectatoring" as a way of delaying their climaxes. "Each time I feel like I'm coming, I try to imagine that I'm just watching this other guy having sex, and that it's not me at all."

Once Sylvia had demonstrated to Barry that he was still capable of achieving erections quite easily, she sat astride him one morning and guided his hardened penis into her vagina. Because she was sitting on top, she could control the pace of their lovemaking, and how deeply his penis penetrated her. This was very important because men with erection problems—afraid that their penis will soften before they can reach a climax—are often panicked into making love like a hundred-meter sprint.

The first few times, Sylvia took his erection inside her and hardly moved at all, eventually taking it out again and continuing to fondle it manually. Again, there was no pressure on him to reach a climax. But it didn't take too long before Barry and Sylvia were back to making love as usual, and Barry had stopped binge drinking. The only difference—"We're much more sexually adventurous these days. After sorting out Barry's erection problems, we feel that we can talk about anything without any inhibitions whatsoever. We tried anal intercourse for the first time. I think Barry wanted to show me that he could get hard enough to do it. I didn't like it too much to begin with, but now that I've gotten used to it, I love it. I like to lie in bed absolutely still, not moving, with Barry's cock buried in my butt.

"I sometimes think what would have happened if we hadn't worked this out. I guess Barry would have gone to a doctor or something, but supposing he hadn't wanted to? When it comes to a relationship between a man and a woman, sex isn't everything, is it? And when it comes to sex, a hard-on isn't everything, is it? But it's pretty difficult to imagine any kind of sex life without it."

In Barry's case, there was nothing seriously wrong

with him, physically or psychologically, but you can see how his erection problems could have led very quickly to a deterioration in his sexual relationship with Sylvia, and their marriage, too. Many otherwise happy relationships are irrevocably torn apart by erectile dysfunction and all the psychological traumas that go with it. Other relationships continue, but only as shells of their former selves, with both partners reconciled to the idea that they are never again going to have the sexual pleasure which they used to enjoy when they first got together.

Not all erection difficulties can be solved at home by do-it-yourself techniques—especially if they are caused by chronic drug or health problems. But if you take the trouble to understand your partner's sexual difficulties, and show willingness to assist him in getting over them, you can literally work wonders. A woman who has helped to restore her partner's ability to get an erection will be rewarded with far more than a nightly hard-on.

She will have developed an intimacy with her partner that can lead to more exciting sex than she ever thought possible. As one woman told me, "These days, when we make love, I almost feel that *I* know what it's like to have an erection."

Even if your lover doesn't have erection problems at all, you can learn to massage and manipulate his penis almost as skillfully as if you were him. It's impossible for one person to know exactly what her partner is feeling when she fondles him. You know this yourself, from your own partner's attempts to stimulate your clitoris. He might have his fingertip close to your most sensitive spot, and he might *nearly* be doing it quickly enough, with *nearly* the right amount of pressure. But don't you sometimes wish that you could tell him to stroke you just a little bit faster, and a little less roughly, and slightly further up, to the left?

You can't know exactly what your partner is feeling when you rub his penis any more than *he* can know what you're feeling when he massages your clitoris. But you can certainly improve your manipulation technique beyond recognition, as well as your confidence, and when it comes to giving a man an erection, it's confidence that counts more than anything. Knowing how hard to grip it, and where; and how quickly to rub it, and when.

In the opening chapter of this book, you will learn how a man's penis grows stiff, and how to hold it and fondle it when it does. But giving a man a rock-hard erection also involves mental empathy—recognizing the rising stages of sexual arousal, knowing what images are likely to be going through your partner's mind as he grows more and more excited. As his climax approaches, you will be able to whisper wilder and dirtier suggestions into his ear, and these will intensify the feelings that you are giving him with your fingers.

When he is only a heartbeat away from ejaculating, you may even be able to hold his penis totally still, and make him climax by words alone. Now, there's an impressive trick.

To be able to control a man's sexual organs as confidently as this, you have to be very familiar with them, and completely unafraid to touch them and manipulate them at any time. It may surprise you, but one of the commonest causes of sexual problems in long-term relationships is that the woman is simply not familiar with her partner's parts . . . even to look at, let alone fondle.

"My husband and I aren't ashamed of being naked in front of one another," said Louise, 34, a print designer from Seattle, Washington. "But I wouldn't actually sit and stare at his cock at close quarters, or start playing around with it just to see what it looked like."

Renata, 28, a musician from Berkeley, California, said, "If I close my eyes and try to picture my boyfriend's penis? No, I don't think I can. I can imagine what it feels like inside me, and I can imagine what it feels like to hold it. But what it actually looks like . . . it sounds crazy, doesn't it, but I'm kind of vague. I think he has a mole near the end. But then penises look different all the time, don't they? One minute they're tiny and the next they're, like, *huge*."

Even among women who had been in sexual relationships with the same man for more than a decade, fewer than 21 percent were sure that they would recognize him by his genitals alone. (By contrast, more than 53 percent of men claimed that they would recognize their partner's vulvas—which is not only an interesting confirmation of the fact that men are much more responsive to visual stimulation than women, but a reminder of the distinctive differences in genitalia from woman to woman. Some women have a more prominent mound of Venus, for example, or fleshier lips, or a more hooded clitoris.)

Many women had the feeling that their partner's genitals were "his property" and were cautious of fondling them unless they were actually making love. Janice, a 26-year-old Realtor from Philadelphia, Pennsylvania, said, "I used to come up behind him in the kitchen when he was cooking, pull down his zipper and play with his cock until it got hard. I used to say, 'What's this? I didn't know we were having zucchini tonight!' But once he was sitting up in bed reading, and I opened up his pajamas and started to masturbate him. I think he must have liked it but he didn't say anything and he didn't go fully hard, so I didn't know what to do. So I stopped. And ever after that, I was kind of confused about touching him. Had I chosen the wrong moment, and if so, what was wrong about it? Maybe I was doing it wrong. It made me very cautious about touching him again."

Janice didn't appreciate that a man's penis won't *always* stiffen when it's manipulated, especially if the man is tired or very relaxed or not in the mood for making love. Her misunderstanding was shared by Sheila, a 35-year-old teacher from Indianapolis, Indiana. "A man's cock is almost like a measuring rod, isn't it, which gives you empirical proof that you're sexy? Yes—I would be concerned if I fondled my partner's penis and it didn't get hard. Maybe not too much, if it only happened once or twice, and I knew the reason why. Say, alcohol, or tiredness, or something like that. But if it happened quite often? I'd begin to think that he was seeing another woman. So—whichever way you look at it—a hard penis is definitely important for a woman's self-esteem."

The simple truth is that a man can still derive enormous pleasure from your fondling his cock and his balls, even if you can't see the evidence of it in a full erection (or if he gets an erection and subsequently loses it, or if he gets an erection but doesn't manage to climax). I have always said that sexual relations can benefit enormously if men and women learn to play with each other's genitals without necessarily feeling that it *has* to lead to intercourse and that intercourse *has* to lead to a climax. That's why I have always been reluctant to use the word "foreplay," because it suggests that genital fondling must inevitably lead to penetration, when of course it doesn't have to, and sometimes it's much more pleasurable if there isn't any pressure to "perform."

Many women have told me that they are often tempted to fondle their partner's penises, or even to give them oral sex, but that they are wary of doing so because their partners will immediately assume they want intercourse. Alyssa, a 35-year-old gardener from Gainesville, Florida, said, "There are so many times when all I want to do is stroke him in a leisurely way and pull his cock up and down and suck his balls. I could do it for *hours* if he'd give me the chance. But the second I touch his cock he seems to take that as a signal that we have to be up and at it. Either that, or he pushes me away and says, 'Not tonight, girl, I'm bushed,' as if I'm expecting him to give me some kind of Olympic-gold-medal fuck every single time we do it. I don't know how to explain to him that all I want to do is give him a long, luxurious *feel*. I tried once but I don't think he understood what I was trying to say. With him, it's either a fuck or it isn't."

In a later chapter, we'll see how you can take away most of the panic that many men feel to "perform," so that you can fondle your partner's penis for as long as you like. As you become more and more familiar with his sexual responses, you will find that you can almost give him erections to order, which is more than he can do.

If he's suffering from erectile dysfunction—whether it's temporary or long-term—we'll also see how "long, luxurious" fondling sessions can gradually help to rebuild his sexual confidence.

For hard, lasting erections, you not only need to know what your partner's penis feels like to you, but what it feels like to *him*. Now, a woman can never completely understand what it's like to have a penis dangling between her legs, any more than a man can completely understand what it's like to have a vagina. But during the preparation of this book I talked to many different men about what it actually feels like to have a penis—especially when it's sexually aroused—and I think that their answers were very helpful and illuminating. Knowing just how little control a man has over his own penis is a revelation to many women. But—once they understand—they are much better equipped to help their partners get hard.

Carl, 27, is an architect from San Diego, California.

He is single, although he has a "kind of steady" girl-friend in Jane, 24, who works in a fashion store. "I don't think that girls fully understand that a guy can get wood whether he wants to or not, and at the same time that he can lose his wood just when he wants it the most. Either way, it can be totally embarrassing.

"The first time I saw Jane was on the beach, and she was wearing this tiny orange string bikini, and when I say tiny I mean microscopic. I couldn't keep my eyes off her. I mean everything about her turned me on. She was blonde, and her skin was honey-brown, and there was sand on the cheeks of her ass. Her breasts are pretty big and whenever she ran across the beach they bounced up and down. And her bikini bottom was so small that you could tell she was totally waxed, you know, and it was tucked up into her pussy, like somebody had pushed it up there with one finger.

"I defy any guy to sit next to a girl like that and not get wood. Because I did. I was wearing these blue check swimshorts and they were pretty baggy, but all the same my cock came up rigid and it wouldn't go down. I tried to think about different types of roofing shingles. I tried to think about pre-stressed concrete. None of it worked, because I couldn't stop myself from looking across at Jane sitting ten yards away from me, rubbing sun cream between her breasts.

"I tried lying facedown but that only m̲___
worse because when you get really hard l̲___
any pressure on your cock only turns yo̲___

more. So I turned over onto my back and there it was—sticking up like a goddamned tent pole. Jane looked my way and so I sat up quickly and pretended I was rummaging around in my sports bag.

"If you asked me to describe to a girl what it's like to get wood, I'd have to say that it's like being stung by a bee . . . your cock swells up and it won't go down, and you have this sensation that's partly pleasurable and partly irritating. Your cock feels incredibly sensitive. Just the way it strains against your shorts makes it tingle. You really want to rub it to relieve that feeling—or, better still, to have sex.

"Also I don't think that girls realize how hard your cock can get. Like, 'wood' is no exaggeration. When I feel really horny, my cock is like it's carved out of solid mahogany, and a girl could squeeze it as tight as she possibly could, and she still couldn't hurt me.

"Your cock will only go down when it decides to go down, and willing it to go down makes absolutely no difference. Actually, it can have the opposite effect, because suddenly you're hyperaware that it's hard and tingly and sticking out the front of your pants and that makes it harder and tinglier still.

"It's the same when you can't get it up. I haven't had that problem too often, knock on wood. Only once or twice, when I've been wiped out by a hangover. But then again, girls don't seem to understand that Mr. Softy will simply not rise to the occasion unless he really wants to. You can concentrate on your cock, for sure. You can try to mind-meld with it, like Mr. Spock in *Star Trek*. I feel horny, and my ·lfriend's panting for it, so rise, damn you, rise!

And what happens? Nothing. All you have between your legs is this wiggly bit of flesh that doesn't even feel like it belongs to you. It's like it's been anesthetized. It's numb."

How did he feel about Jane's confidence in fondling his genitals?

"Oh, I don't think she's afraid to do it. She likes to do it, especially when we're taking a shower together. You know, the soap job. But even then I don't think she completely understands the effect that she has on me, when she fondles me. Like, she rubs my cock in the shower and I'm starting to get that clenched-tight feeling between my legs, like it wouldn't take very much more rubbing to make me come, but then she suddenly stops doing it and gets out of the shower and I'm left standing there feeling let down to say the least. There's not even any guarantee that she's going to continue doing it in the bedroom. She'll, like, put on her robe and start to blow her hair dry, while I'm standing there with my cock sticking out like an Apollo rocket and what does she do? She smiles at me, and goes on drying her hair. I mean—I'm not blaming her, it's as much my fault as it is hers, for not explaining how I feel. But somehow it kind of destroys the spontaneity, saying, 'Go on! Go on! Rub me harder!' "

Carl felt that girls could enjoy sex very much more if they had more understanding of how men physically feel. "The way I see it, there's always been this thing that the guy's in control, setting the pace. But I don't think that always makes for the best sex. I once went out with a French girl and she wouldn't let me put my cock inside her for what seemed like hours . . . she kept kissing me and teasing me and digging her claws in my balls, but every time I tried to push myself into her, she covered her pussy with her hand and wouldn't let me in. Talk about frustrating, you know? But when it did happen . . . well, it was something else. She let me inside her about a sixteenth of an inch at a time, and when I *was* in, she made sure that we did it real slow and easy. A couple of times I tried to go faster but when I did she took my cock out and held it tight, until I got the message that she wanted it to last. It seemed like it went on forever, but in the end we both climaxed. She came first, and then me right afterward, and believe me we savored every last twitch. I mean, we were going 'Ahhhh . . .' and 'Mmmhhh . . .' like we'd just finished a really great meal.''

Phil, 29, a sound technician from Gainesville, Florida, has always treated his penis as if it has a separate life of its own. In fact he regards it as a pet and calls it "Norris." "Girls never give me a hard time if Norris can't come out to play for any particular reason. They know that *I'm* really hot to do the wild thing, okay, but they accept the fact that Norris has a hangover or maybe he's just too tired.

"On the other hand, if Norris refuses to behave himself and keeps standing up and begging for it, then I don't feel that I have to apologize. I just say, 'Gee, Charlene, Norris really, really likes you, what can I say?' "

The way that Phil talks about his penis may seem like a joke, but it's a joke that enables his girlfriends to understand that men have very little conscious control over their erections, and that there are times when a man can't manage to raise an erection even though he would gladly sign over everything he owns in exchange for twenty minutes of total hardness. Similarly, if he finds a girl sexually attractive, and his penis responds by getting erect, there is no way that he can make it curl up simply by wishing it would.

"Most girls really get into the Norris thing, because they can treat him like a pet, and stroke him, and sometimes they even talk to him, and somehow they don't seem so shy about playing with my cock because he has a personality of his own. I've even had them opening up my zipper and putting their hand in my pants and saying, 'Isn't Norris coming out today?' And they really get a kick out of making Norris grow big. Like, 'Look at you now, Norris, you're *enormous*!'"

The "Norris" game works because many women can be shy of their partner's genitals, and unsure about handling them or what to call them. These days sex is freely and openly discussed in women's-interest magazines, but the reality of a man's penis and how it works is very different from a diagram on a printed page. Many women complain to me that the sexual instruction that they received at school was "helpful, but not *hands-on*." As Phoebe, a 29-year-old publishing assistant from New York City, remarked, "It was like being told everything about babies, but not what it's actually like to hold one. Babies are wriggly and awkward and you never know if you're holding them properly." In the same way, your partner's sex organs can be soft or hard, squirmy or rigid, a battering ram one minute and a sensitive orchid the next. So how do you learn how to handle them?

Janet, a 24-year-old hair stylist from Schaumburg, Illinois, said, "My mother told me all about men getting hard, and all about condoms, and making sure I didn't get pregnant. She was quite liberated and she even told me about oral sex and anal sex and sexual fantasies. But she never explained to me what it was that men expect you to do with their cocks. I always got the feeling when I went to bed with a guy that he wanted something with his cock and I didn't know what it was."

One of the problems is that many men find it difficult to tell their partners what kind of stimulation they want. "What am I supposed to say?" asked Ben, 27, a trainee attorney. " 'Okay, doll—you can suck my cock now,' and wave it in front of her face? And what if she sucks it but she isn't doing it right? If a girl doesn't suck your cock right you hardly feel anything except wet. What can I say without upsetting her?" Another difficulty is explaining to a woman how arousing it can be for a man to have his testes fondled—and how agonizing it can be if she's just a little too enthusiastic.

If a man has trouble in getting erections, he can find it very much more difficult to describe what kind of stimulation he wants. Embarrassed by his lack of potency, he would rather blame drink or tiredness or stress and say "Let's try again in the morning"—rather than encourage his partner to take hold of his penis and fondle him back to full hardness—even when there is a reasonable possibility that she could.

It is always important that sexual glitches are dealt with honestly and openly and *as soon as you possibly can*. Few problems have the potential for damaging an intimate relationship like erection problems, because they carry all the associated baggage of male pride and female self-esteem. However tolerant and sophisticated we are these days about sexual dysfunction, we still think that erections *define* our sexual relationships: a hard cock shows that a man is healthy and strong and dominant, and that his woman is highly desirable. As soon as his erections start to fail, those definitions are immediately brought into question. A man who can't get an erection thinks of himself as much less of a man, while a woman who can't make her partner's penis go hard thinks of herself as less attractive. The consequences can be disastrous.

However, they needn't be. You can acquire the power and the knowledge to revive your partner's penis if it's started to show signs of flagging. You can give it all-night durability even if it's still in first-class working order.

Very often, a couple who manage to overcome erection problems together become very much more intimate and share a depth of sexual understanding which they never had before. So even if you're frustrated, or close to despair, you should think of the challenge that you and your partner are facing as a new beginning.

Believe me, there's no way to go but up.

Quiz:

A Hard Day's Night?

These are some of the questions that women most frequently ask me about their lovers' erections.

Q: My partner hasn't made love to me for weeks. Do you think he doesn't find me so attractive any more? A: If your partner appears to be avoiding sex, then it is highly likely that he is suffering from erection problems. He is reluctant to tell you that something is wrong and he is probably hoping against hope that the condition will eventually cure itself. Is he staying up unusually late, so that when he eventually comes to bed you are both too tired to make love? Does he claim that his work is extra stressful at the moment, or that he is worried about his career, or money, or some other problem unrelated to sex, and that this is the reason he doesn't feel like making love?

Your first reaction is to feel rejected—and very understandably. Maybe you suspect that he might be having an affair with another woman. You may even think that he could be gay. But the chances are that

he has a simple physical problem which will be very
easy to deal with, especially if you give him sympa-
thy and help. Stop worrying that you've lost your
allure (because you probably haven't) and ask him
outright if he's having any trouble getting erections.
No matter how macho a man is, erection problems
are almost impossible for him to deal with on his
own, and trying to hide them almost always makes
them worse.

Q: My new lover has a much shorter penis than any
man I have slept with before. He is very self-
conscious about it. He tries to avoid getting undressed in front of me and every time we make love
he asks me if he has satisfied me. I tell him yes
(which is true) but I don't think he believes me. Now
he has started to have trouble getting an erection. Is
there anything that I can do?
A: It's surprising how many men worry about the
size of their penis, whereas almost all of them are
perfectly normal. The average length of a young
man's penis is 4–7 inches (102–178mm) and it is technique rather than size that satisfies his partner during
intercourse. You should talk to him about his anxiety,
and openly fondle his genitals and show him how
much you like doing it. Show relish for his cock so
that he can see that you're not concerned about how
short it is. There's no point in trying to pretend that
his penis is bigger than it really is, but as long as
you can convince him that you prefer his cock to any
other, you'll go a long way toward dispelling his
anxiety. If you still can't shake him out of it, encour-

age him to visit his doctor for professional reassurance that his penis is more than long enough.

Q: My boyfriend is a terrific footballer and very fit, but every weekend he drinks too much and he can never manage to get an erection. He says he needs to drink to let off steam but I'm beginning to worry because our sex life is suffering.

A: In limited quantities, booze can lower your sexual inhibitions and make sexual intercourse more likely. But large amounts of alcohol can make it impossible for a man to get or keep an erection—the so-called brewer's droop—and a man who regularly drinks to excess over a number of years may permanently impair his sexual performance. If your boyfriend stops drinking so much, he will probably be able to perform, but you ought to ask him to think seriously about the damage that he is doing both to your relationship and to his liver. Quite frankly, he sounds as if he is too immature to worry too much about either. Find a football player who prefers sex to suds.

Q: Whenever we date, my boyfriend seems to have an almost permanent hard-on. He is always giving me intimate caresses when nobody is looking and rubbing his erection up against me. I've never experienced this before and I'm wondering if there's something wrong with him.

A: Lucky you. Your boyfriend clearly finds you very sexy, and he is eager to show you what effect you have on his penis. An unduly prolonged erection is known as **priapism** and is usually a rare side effect of some antidepressant drugs like Prozac, or because some treatment for impotence has worked rather too well. In its early stages, a prolonged erection can often be treated by a cold bath or the application of a bag of frozen peas. But if it persists for three to four hours it can become very painful, and you need to seek medical assistance. In your case, a short burst of energetic sexual activity should do the trick.

Q: I met my new lover at a business conference. He is a married man who heads up a large international corporation—handsome, dynamic, and very charismatic. He is the first man I have ever slept with who is uncircumcised. Lately, however, he has been having difficulty in getting erections when we make love, and since you stress that impotence is usually caused by simple physical problems, could it be that his foreskin makes his penis less sensitive?

A: I'm afraid you're deliberately closing your eyes to the blindingly obvious likelihood that his impotence is caused by guilt. When an uncircumcised man has a hard-on, his foreskin automatically peels back so that the head of his penis is exposed, and so it has no effect whatsoever on erotic sensitivity. There have been arguments since time immemorial about the relative sensitivity of circumcised and uncircumcised penises, and although it could be claimed that a circumcised penis, since it is permanently exposed to friction, might lose some of its "touchy-feeliness," I have never met a circumcised man who complained about it. You'll have to talk to your lover about his problem and be prepared to face up to the fact that

his infidelity is preying on his mind and affecting his
ability to get hard.

Q: My husband and I have been together for twenty-
one years. Recently he has shown much less interest
in sex than me, and even when I cuddle up to him
in bed and fondle his penis he doesn't often get an
erection. He still says that he loves me, but I'm not
sure that he finds me sexually desirable any more.
A: One of God's more baffling jokes is that men reach
the zenith of their sexual drive at the age of 18, while
women are at their peak, sexually speaking, between
the ages of 35–40. This often causes a woman to believe that her long-term partner has lost interest in
her—especially when she thinks back on how horny
he was when they first dated. If he says he still loves
you, then he probably does, but you will need to
coax him into getting back into the habit of making
love more frequently. It's possible that he may be
suffering from anxiety about his ability to get an erection, or that he's taking some medication that affects
his potency. He may have a physical condition that
needs the attention of a doctor. Discuss your feelings
and your sexual needs, and reassure him that he still
has the wherewithal to satisfy you. The chances are
that he's simply fallen out of practice, and grown
sexually lazy. It sometimes happens that a couple's
sex life takes a backseat for years while they bring
up children, and that sexual problems only become
apparent when they have the time and the privacy
to make love the way they used to. Don't suffer in

silence . . . you deserve an active sex life, an[...]
husband is probably the man who can give it to [...]

Q: The new man in my life is recently divorced. He
is only 36 years old but lately he has been having
trouble making love to me, i.e. not getting erections.
I have told him not to worry and have tried to be
sympathetic because I love him very much. All the
same I am slightly worried that he may be having
second thoughts about us.

A: Divorce is shattering, and even though he may
appear to have survived his ordeal in one piece, your
new partner is still one of the walking wounded.
Whatever caused the split between himself and his
wife, there was bound to have been a great deal of
acrimony and pain on both sides, and he will be
understandably cautious about making a new commitment. He will tell you how devoted he is, and
that he is prepared to spend the rest of his life with
you, and he may very well believe it. But his subcon-
scious will be warning him not to make the same
mistake again. Be patient, and give him time, and
don't allow your sexual enthusiasm to wane. Keep
up those caresses and those intimate fondles, even
when he gets the flops, and show him that he's not
going to lose *you* that easily.

Q: The man in my life has put on quite a bit of
weight. I don't mind him being bulkier, but his penis
has shrunk.

A: I'm not going to bang on about excess weight

being unhealthy. You get enough of that in diet books, and I have met scores of "overweight" couples who have truly amazing sex lives. Weight is only a sexual problem if it prevents you from having satisfying intercourse, or if you find yourself short of breath or suffering from heart palpitations when you make love. Some men complain that their penises seem to diminish as they grow older, but this is probably because the muscles and fibers become less elastic with age. I doubt if your man's penis has *really* shrunk. It seems much more likely that fatty tissue has accumulated around the base of his penis, like a chubby baby's, which simply gives you the visual impression that his penis is smaller. The only solution is to stay away from double cheeseburgers.

Q: My partner has been suffering from erection problems for over a year. He says he doesn't want to leave me but has suggested that if we both had affairs it might give our sex life some new excitement. I don't want to have an affair, but do you think it would help us if I allowed him to have sex with another woman?

A: Very bad idea, both for him and for you, and for the survival of your relationship. If he's having erection problems but seriously doesn't want to leave you, then you both need to find out what's causing them, and see what you can do to sort them out. There could be something physically wrong with him that calls for medical attention. If he really loves you, an affair won't cure genuine erection problems. It will probably make them worse, because he will feel guilty about what he is doing, and if he fails to get an erection with another woman, his "fear of failure" will be doubly compounded. Try to rekindle your sex life with the techniques you learn from this book. If none of them work, I think you will have to admit that he doesn't love you as much as he protests, and that he wants to stay with you simply because it is comfortable and convenient.

Q: I am 51 and have started hormone replacement therapy. I can't stop thinking about sex and I feel like having it almost every night. However, my husband is not so enthusiastic and lately he has been unable to get an erection, which is frustrating me so much that I don't know what to do.

A: Hormone replacement therapy (HRT) often has the effect of hotting up a woman's sexual desire. The problem is that men can feel threatened by their partner's newly rekindled lust and become worried that they won't be up to satisfying it. The result is the usual trouble: anxiety causes erectile dysfunction which causes anxiety which causes further erectile dysfunction. You need to make it absolutely clear to your husband that your passions have been aroused by your therapy, and that he is more than man enough for you. Remind him of the reasons you took HRT to begin with—the moods, the night sweats, the vaginal dryness—and explain that if increased sexiness is the only side effect, then there's not very much for him to worry about. Treat your excess libido as fun, and encourage him to satisfy you in other ways—with his fingers, or with his tongue, or with sex toys. If you don't put him under any pressure to produce an erection every time you have hanky-panky, you'll find that he will soon be getting hard of his own accord. In fact, your HRT may very well make a new man of him.

Q: My partner doesn't feel like sex very often and when we do make love he often loses his erection halfway through. He gets angry if I try to talk about it. Is there something I can put in his food to increase his sex drive?

A: The short answer to that is no. You should never give anybody any kind of additive to food or drink without their knowledge. If they have allergies, it could prove dangerous or fatal. Apart from that, there is no known substance which has been medically proven to increase sexual performance. There is no such thing as a genuine aphrodisiac, either, no matter what you read in the newspapers about "Valentine's Day Dinners" of oysters and champagne. If there is any sexual effect, it's all in the mind. It sounds as if your partner has a genuine sexual problem which he needs to discuss with a doctor. Is he depressed about something? Is he taking any medication? Even if he gets angry, try to persuade him that he ought to seek professional help. Invent a girlfriend whose partner suffered the same problem, and tell him that once this imaginary partner had talked to a doctor, he was cured within a couple of weeks. Show him plenty of physical affection as well as encouragement. Men who suffer from impotence will often avoid sexual contact so that they won't be humiliated by failing to get an erection, but at the same time they badly miss the warmth and intimacy of a cuddle.

Q: My girlfriend says that she sat on her boyfriend's penis and broke it. Is this possible or is she just telling a story?
A: A man's erect penis can be "broken" if you put too much weight on it. This sometimes happens if a couple is having vigorous intercourse at an awkward angle, or if—like your girlfriend—a woman accidentally sits on it. The fibers inside the penis are torn, and the pain is eye-watering, to say the least. If this happens, a man needs urgent medical attention. He will heal, slowly, but he will avoid its happening again.

Q: My boyfriend's penis gets bigger when we make love but never gets totally rigid. A friend of mine says he should put it into a bottle to stop the blood flowing out and to give him a really hard erection.
A: A man should never, ever insert his penis into a bottle. He may get a really hard erection, but he will suffer considerable pain and he won't be able to get his penis out until the bottle is smashed. I have talked to doctors in emergency rooms in many different countries, and the variety of constricting objects which men have placed around their penises in order to maintain a really hard erection is mind-boggling—such as ivory napkin rings, plastic hosepipe connectors, key rings, scissor handles, wristwatch bezels, photograph frames and vacuum-cleaner nozzles. One

man even tied a nylon strap around the base of his penis—the kind that is used for fastening hoses in auto engines, and which have irreversible teeth. His penis swelled, burying the strap in distended flesh, and it took several agonizing hours in the ER to cut the strap off. The rule is simple: never place *anything* around a man's penis that you won't be able to remove once he's erect. As we shall see later, there are several constricting rings on the market which are specifically designed to retain erections, but all of these can be easily taken off afterward.

Q: My partner is a terrific guy, and we make love three or four times a week at least. He doesn't have any difficulty in getting an erection, but he always climaxes much too soon for me. It seems like he's only inside me for two or three minutes before he ejaculates. I have managed to get him to spend more time on sexual play, before we actually have intercourse, and twice I have *nearly* managed to have an orgasm with his penis inside me. However, this was only because he had almost brought me to orgasm already, with his tongue. Is there anything I can do to make him last longer?

A: In my opinion the Western idea of sexual satisfaction is centered far too much on the importance of reaching a climax. Too many men think of sexual intercourse as if it's the Kentucky Derby and they have to be first past the post. Obviously there is something wrong if a man is unable to reach a climax, or to sustain an erection long enough to ejaculate, and these are problems which we will be looking at later. As far as your partner is concerned, there are several tried-and-tested ways to delay his climax, in particular the "squeeze technique" which Masters and Johnson initiated for the treatment of premature ejaculation. But in conjunction with these methods, it is important for you to introduce the idea into your lovemaking that it is the pleasure of the journey which matters, whether you arrive or not. Most men feel that if they don't ejaculate, their virility is somehow in question, a feeling which is reinforced by pornographic movies and magazines, in which intercourse invariably ends up with a copious shooting-out of sperm, usually over faces or breasts. Not only that, the biological purpose of intercourse is to make a woman pregnant, and so men have a natural urge not only to climax, but to climax ASAP. However, men should remember that pornographic movies, like any other kinds of movies, are for entertainment purposes only, and that they are not the best guides to making love . . . any more than *The Fast and the Furious* was the best guide to urban driving. And as far as their reproductive urges are concerned, there is no desperate urgency to increase the world population—not this year, anyhow. With your help, your partner can learn to throttle back his sexual drive and channel it into creative play. Of course there will always be occasions when you both feel like a quick, furious fuck, but your partner needs to understand that most of the time you want your lovemaking to last, so that you can savor the feeling of having him inside you. You will have to find a way to talk to him about this. Make it clear that there is nothing lacking in his virility. In fact, you can tell him that he's just a little *too* virile, and that's why he needs to slow down. Introduce him to some of the exercises in this book, and after a little practice I think you'll find that he's capable of holding back his climax long enough for you to climax first, while his penis is still inside you, and still hard.

Q: About eighteen months ago, my partner started to have trouble in keeping his erection for long enough to reach a climax. His problem has grown steadily worse, and now he hardly ever gets an erection at all. I have tried to be understanding but I have not been able to help him very much, and he refuses to go to his doctor. I am beginning to feel that our relationship is falling apart, and these days we are always arguing.

A: Read this book and encourage your partner to read it, too. Try the techniques I describe and if your partner has no serious psychological or medical problems, they should help you to overcome his problems completely. If they don't, then he really has to bite the bullet and seek guidance from his doctor. Most men find it extremely difficult to admit to any problems "down there." Some men even ignore lumps in their testicles because they're too embarrassed to seek professional guidance. But your partner should know that one in ten men suffer from ED at some time or another, and doctors are quite used to dealing with it, whether it's caused by anxiety or alcohol or drugs, or simply by a lack of sexual confidence. Reassure your partner that most of the cures for erection problems are extremely simple and effective, and that once his penis is back in full working order, he'll feel like making love to you three times a night, every night. Whether your relationship can survive that— well, that's your problem.

Q: My husband has never been particularly "well endowed" even though our sex life has never given me anything to complain about. Last week, when my girlfriends got together, we watched a porno video, and one of the men in it had a huge cock that must have been about 10 inches long. I can't stop myself from fantasizing about it, and wishing that my husband's cock was bigger. Is there any way of enlarging a man's penis?

A: There are five ways in which men attempt to enlarge their penises: by natural exercise, by regularly using a vacuum pump, by taking herbal pills, by surgery and (believe it or not) by hanging weights on them. Natural exercise is very pleasurable but the penis is not a muscle and cannot be made to bulge like a bodybuilder's biceps. Vacuum pumps can increase penis size but only temporarily and at some risk of rupturing blood vessels and causing lymphatic blisters, although they can be useful in overcoming erectile dysfunction. Herbal pills may have other beneficial effects but enlarging a man's penis is not one of them. Surgery can physically make a penis larger, but there is a high risk of unsightly scarring, impaired sensitivity and a penis that is inherently unstable. Hanging weights on a penis can increase its length, but as any experienced Play-Doh modeler can tell you, length can only be acquired at the expense of thickness . . . so only go for the weights option if you don't mind your husband having a pencil-willy.

Out of the hundreds of questions that women have sent me about their partners' sexual performance, these are some of the most frequently asked. Of course every sexual relationship is different and every man's sexual responses are individual, but you will find in this book most of the basic techniques for keeping your man hard and happy, and I am sure that you have more than enough imagination to adapt them to your own particular needs. Even if your partner is suffering from a health problem which can be effectively treated by his doctor, you can help his recovery in all kinds of creative and exciting ways . . . and if he is perfectly healthy, you can improve his staying power so that you can both enjoy the kind of love life that you always dreamed about.

One: "Ten-Hut!"

How Erections Happen

Considering that a fully functioning penis is the single most important thing in a couple's sex life, it is amazing how many women have no idea how or why it gets erect.

Men get erections spontaneously, especially when they're dreaming, and when they first wake up in the morning. German researchers have worked out that the average man of 70 has spent thirty-three thousand hours of his life with a hard-on—or roughly three years, nine months and a few stiff weeks. This isn't counting the number of erections he has had when masturbating or making love.

"Of course we were taught about men's anatomy at school," said 26-year-old Heidi, a beautician from Orlando, Florida. "But at that age you're kind of embarrassed about it, and it doesn't really sink in. Not only that, the diagrams are all, like, scientific, and you can't really associate them with the tent pole that you can see in the front of your boyfriend's swimming shorts."

All the same, the tent pole in the front of your boyfriend's swimming shorts is *very* scientific. It's caused by a fascinating combination of biology, chemistry and psychology, and the more you know about it, the more tent poles you'll be able to coax out of him. That's why I said in the foreword to this book that in order to get the best out of your man's penis, you'll have to start thinking a little bit technical. Sex is moonlight and roses and seductive music, but it's also nerves and arteries and blood flow.

Let's pretend that you have your partner lying beside you, and that he's naked. On the other hand, don't let's pretend—why don't you ask him to strip off and lie beside you for real? If you can persuade him to assist you in your discovery of what makes his penis work, then there will be tremendous benefits for both of you. You shouldn't find it too difficult to enlist his help: he won't have to do anything but lie there while you fondle his penis and his testicles.

If he can't or won't do it, however, don't worry. You can just imagine that he's there . . . or maybe you can imagine that some other man has agreed to help you. Some tall, tanned athlete with a six-pack, and a penis that's a couple of inches longer. Your partner won't find out, will he?

When they're soft, men's penises can vary in size from slightly under 3 inches to 4½ inches long, and about 3–4½ inches in circumference. Take a fabric tape measure and check for yourself what this actually looks like.

When they're erect, penises range from 4½ inches to 8¼ inches in length, and about 3½ to 4¼ inches in circumference. The majority of men are about 6 inches long, give or take a few sixteenths.

Of course there are always exceptions. During my career as editor of *Penthouse* and *Penthouse Forum* magazines, as well as executive editor of the Swedish sex magazine *Private,* I met a number of men whose penises were simply enormous. One of them was nearly 15 inches in length when erect, with a girth of 6¼ inches. The girls with whom he had sex for pornographic pictures reacted with awe, and they particularly enjoyed the challenge of taking his erection as far down their throats as they could, even when he almost choked them. The men with whom he posed all pretended that they didn't care that he was hung like a horse, although they were obviously jealous and felt that their own penises, by comparison, were puny.

One model, Bjorn, told me, "I hate that guy so much. I stand next to him naked and instantly he makes me feel like I couldn't even satisfy a lady mouse. He never says a word, but I always think that he's looking down at my tiny little dick and thinking, 'What woman can possibly be turned on by *that*?' It was a terrible, terrible feeling, even worse than sitting in traffic in a crummy secondhand Beetle and some guy draws up next to you in a Ferrari. At least when that happens you can think to yourself, 'One day, you bastard, I'll be able to buy a Ferrari, too.' But I know for sure that I'm never going to look down between my legs and see a 15-inch cock sticking up."

We'll get into penis enlargement later in this book,

but I want to talk about size because it's one of the most important aspects of a man's sense of sexual self-worth, and also one of the most misunderstood. Fact: the size of your partner's penis has little or no effect on his ability to stimulate you and satisfy you. Deep penetration may be thrilling, but a man with a smaller penis is perfectly equipped to bring you to orgasm.

However, let's be honest about it: many women are excited by very large penises. As Gary Griffin, the editor of *Penis Power Quarterly*, said, "There's no logic behind it . . . it's the visual perception." A very large penis makes a man look more virile, and holds out the promise that any woman he makes love to will be totally satisfied. Gina, a 31-year-old tennis coach from San Diego, California, said, "I went into Grant's room to borrow one of his rackets without realizing that he was there. He stepped out of the bathroom naked, toweling his hair. I couldn't help looking at his cock. It was enormous, bigger than any cock that I'd ever seen before, hanging almost down to his knees. And thick, too. It looked as if I would have had trouble closing my hand around it. He had blond pubic curls, neatly trimmed, and big heavy balls. I only saw him for a second, because he covered himself with his towel, but that second was enough for me to have a clear mental picture. I fantasized about him all day, and when I went to bed that night I was still thinking about his cock, and how big it must have been when it was hard. I could imagine myself sucking that huge purple head, and then lying on my back and opening my legs up as wide as I possibly could, so that he could push his cock into me, and fill me up so much that I couldn't take another inch of cock if I tried."

But there's a difference between fantasy and reality, which most women are sensible enough to accept, and very few of them complain about the size of their current partner's penis. In the same way, many men are turned on by girls with very big breasts, but are perfectly content for their partner to remain a 34B.

Many of the great seducers of history only had very average equipment—Casanova, for example. And if you're interested, there is a list on the Internet of the comparative sizes of rock stars' penises, based on firsthand observation. You'd be surprised how many of them rate as "small," "short," or "average"— but that certainly doesn't affect their desirability, or their performance in the sack. Some of the wildest rockers rate as "very considerate" when it comes to satisfying their partners in bed, and that's much more important than having a huge penis.

Most of the men who are seriously unhappy about the size of their penises are suffering from the same feeling of inadequacy as my friend Bjorn. They're not worried about their ability to satisfy the woman they're sleeping with. What *does* concern them is their appearance in the locker room, where machismo and self-image are at stake. A study in South Africa by doctors Roos and Lissoos showed that "most patients confessed that their fears and anxieties about their penis size had sprung not from the reaction of women during sexual relationships, but from the denigrating behavior of other males."

They asked their patients why they wanted bigger penises, and 79 percent answered that it was for self-image while only 14 percent said that they wanted to improve their sex lives.

You should be aware how sensitive men can be about the size of their equipment, and how they tend to lack any sense of humor when it comes to other men with larger equipment than theirs. In other words, you need to be a little diplomatic if the subject of penis size ever comes up, and there's never any harm in giving your lover a compliment about his huge erection. "Oh God, you're *enormous!*" never went amiss. "I never realized that men could get as big as this" isn't a bad one, either, especially if he's one of those men who still harbors niggling jealousies about your previous beaux. That remark will wipe out all thoughts of your ex's sexual prowess in one.

A few men become so worried that their penises are undersized—whether it's true or not—that their sexual performance can be affected. If you know or suspect that your lover is suffering from "small penis syndrome," as it's called, there are a number of things you can do to put his mind at rest. One of these is out-and-out deception, I'm afraid, but it works so well that I never hesitate to recommend it. You can "exercise" his penis—either by hand or by using one of the numerous mechanical aids on the market. Then, day by day, you can assure him that his penis is looking and feeling bigger. I promise you that he won't complain about this treatment, and it can be very rewarding for you, too. He'll want to do *something* with that erection you give him.

All through the ages, in different cultures across the world, men have sought to enlarge their penises—not always for the same reason. The Indian sadhus and the Peruvian Cholomecs used weights hanging from their penises to stretch them to lengths of 18–20 inches. They were remarkably long, but as I have mentioned earlier, the penis is not a muscle, and so they ended up remarkably skinny, too. The men couldn't use their penises for anything other than urinating, but I expect that their friends were jealous that they could tuck them into the tops of their socks.

In Brazil in the sixteenth century, the Topinama Indians found a way to enlarge their erections to immense sizes by encouraging poisonous snakes to bite their penises. Like the first man to eat an oyster, it makes you wonder who was mad enough to try it first. According to historical records the Topinamas suffered eye-watering pain for six months, but at the end of that time their penises were absolutely monstrous, and their women were delighted.

So what do women really think about the size of their lovers' penises? Unfortunately, there has been very little serious research on the subject, and most of the surveys are wildly contradictory. Dolores E. Keller, Ph.D., conducted interviews with fifty-seven sexually active women, ranging in age from 17 to 52. Between them, the women had averaged 4.2 partners over a two-year period. Fifty-one of them said they were "more stimulated either by the physical presence of, or fantasized pleasure of, the bigger penis." But note the phrase *"or fantasized pleasure of."* We all have sexual fantasies that are larger than life, but that doesn't mean that we're dissatisfied with what we've got.

Dr. Maj-Britt Rosenbaum believes that "penis size ranks fairly low on most women's lists of physical attributes important to sexual attraction," while Liz McKinnon, writing in *Penis Enlargement Magazine,* said, "I can't really comment objectively on the male desire to possess a huge penis. I once dated a man who dreamed of owning a 'twelve-inch cock.' Come on, let's be real! Twelve inches? What woman could handle anything that large? I understand that there are women who prefer a big penis. But what good is owning an oversized Cadillac when your garage can only accommodate a Volvo?

"Personally, I like the feeling of 'fullness' when a man is inside me. And I'm more of a width-gal than a length-gal . . . that is, I prefer a man who is wider than longer. However, I would never dismiss a man from my bed because of his penis size. It's a cliché to say it but 'It's not the size of the tool, it's how you use it.' There's a lot of truth to that. I've been with small men before. *Really* small! And I was still able to achieve an orgasm."

In my thirty-three years of experience as a sex counselor, I have come across a considerable number of men who have thought that their penises were too short or too small. It was interesting, however, that the women in their lives hadn't even noticed their shortcomings—or, if they had, they hadn't considered for a moment that they were any less sexually attractive, or any less exciting in bed.

Of course it's very hard to convince a man who believes that his penis is too small that he has nothing to worry about. It's a question of self-image—just like some women fret about their size, even though they may be only two or three pounds over their ideal weight. As Liz McKinnon said, "I'm frequently amazed at the females I meet who are totally obsessed with breast enlargement. Women who should know better. Women whom I otherwise respect. Women who already have big breasts, for God's sake! Is this the age we live in . . . a society whose motto screams out, 'If it's bigger, it's better!'?"

As you lie next to your partner and fondle his penis and his testicles, you can do a great deal to bolster his sexual self-confidence by paying him compliments and showing him that his sexual organs are both impressive and fascinating. Many women give their partner's penises a pet name (after all, "I love sucking your penis" does sound rather formal). But take care when choosing a name. Men may make coarse jokes about penises but when it comes to their own, their sensitivity is unbelievable. One of our *Penthouse* models seriously upset her (rather older) lover by calling his penis a "dinkle." Any soubriquet that suggests enormous size will go down well. Xaviera Hollander, the "Happy Hooker," once told me that she called *every* lover's penis "Mr. Big." "It didn't matter if his cock was quite small. It was always 'Mr. Big,' because when he was making love it was the most important part of his body."

Of course there are scores of slang names to choose from, such as cock, dick, dong, prong, schlong, pecker, rocket, wiener, bishop, poker, pole, sausage and knob. I once knew a French girl who always referred to it as "Monsieur Baguette."

However big or small your lover's penis is, it will be constructed in the same way. Take it in your hand and gently stretch it out—or imagine that you are. It is made up of three cylindrical columns of tissue—two larger columns on either side, known as the corpora cavernosa, or "cavernous bodies"—and a narrower column that runs up the underside, the corpus spongiosum or "spongy body."

Normally, the blood vessels inside your lover's penis are constricted, so that very little blood flows into it, and it remains floppy. When he becomes sexually excited, however, his brain releases chemicals which quickly reverse this condition. The blood vessels open wide, blood is pumped into the three columns of tissue, and up it goes.

Inside the corpora cavernosa there are thousands of tiny compartments made up of smooth muscle, and erection occurs when these relax and become filled up with blood. They are all contained in a thick, fibrous envelope called the tunica albuginea, which stretches when your lover's penis becomes erect and prevents all of the blood from draining away again.

On the underside of his penis, the corpus spongiosum surrounds his urethra—the tube through which he pees and shoots out sperm. This column of tissue runs right up to the end of his penis and expands to form the bell-shaped glans—the head of his penis—which is the most sensitive part of his genitals. If you very lightly scratch your lover's penis with your fingernails, you will soon discover that he derives more pleasure from having the underside of his penis tickled than he does from the top. Not unlike scratching a spaniel's chin, really.

Once you have aroused your lover's penis into an erection, you will clearly be able to feel the three columns of blood-filled tissue, like separate ridges. You will also find it easier to examine the opening in his glans. If you gently squeeze his glans, his urethra will gape open and you will be able to see what it looks like. There is no purpose in this except to satisfy your own sexual curiosity. It's important for your self-assurance that you know exactly what every detail of your lover's sexual organs looks like and how they respond to touch. A small word of warning, however. Some women are tempted to arouse their partners by inserting objects into their urethras (such as cotton swabs, lubricated with Vaseline, or even larger objects, such as chopsticks). This is a very dangerous practice which can lead to injury or serious infection. The rule with all sexual play is: treat your bodies with respect.

About a quarter inch beneath the urethral opening is a thin web of connecting skin called the frenum. This spot is highly erogenous, and there aren't many men on the planet who don't enjoy its being gently stroked or licked with the tip of a tongue. We will see later that some men even like to pierce it with rings or studs, supposedly to intensify their sexual pleasure and to give their partners extra vaginal thrills.

Now that your partner's penis is erect, you won't fail to notice a large blue vein running down the top side of it. This is the main vein which empties the blood from his penis once he climaxes, or once he is no longer stimulated.

You should take your time examining his penis. When it's soft, try squeezing it and stretching it, just to get a feel of it. If he has a foreskin, roll it backward and forward. See how many fingertips you can get inside his foreskin. Bite it with your teeth and see how far you can stretch it before he says "Owww!"

There have been furious arguments about foreskins for centuries. Jews, Muslims and Australian Aborigines are ritually circumcised for religious reasons, and at various times in history circumcision has been practiced in most parts of the world—with the exception of Mongols, Hindus, Finns, Hungarians and most Germanic peoples. It is still widespread in North America, although very much less than it used to be.

Circumcision is sometimes considered necessary because a boy's foreskin is too tight, and becomes infected, but this problem can almost always be solved by the application of antiseptic cream. At birth the foreskin and the end of the penis are joined, and it is only during the first three years of life that they become gradually separated. Well-meaning mothers sometimes try to stretch their child's foreskin by pulling it back too far. This can tear the delicate skin and cause scarring, which creates the very condition that they were trying to prevent, and can only be rectified by circumcision.

These days, the arguments in favor of circumcision for reasons of hygiene are largely irrelevant. Most men shower every day, and it only takes a quick pullback of the foreskin to clean it thoroughly underneath. The eminent British pediatrician Sir James Spence famously wrote, "If you show a good reason why a ritual designed to ease the penalties of concupiscence amidst the sand and flies of the Syrian deserts should be continued in this country of clean bed linen and lesser opportunity, I shall listen to your arguments; but if you base your argument on anatomic faults, then I must refute it. Nature is a possessive mistress and you can be sure that she knows best about the genital organs."

Some men claim that a circumcised man can satisfy a woman better because his glans is less sensitive, having been rubbing against his shorts all his life, and so it takes longer for him to reach an orgasm. Not only that, many women say that they find the exposed knob of a circumcised penis more exciting to look at.

But Masters and Johnson showed categorically that there is no difference in the time that it takes circumcised and uncircumcised men to climax—and just as many women say that they are turned on by the way in which the foreskin rolls back when their lover becomes erect.

In sum, to circumcise or not to circumcise is a matter of religious belief and of personal choice. If religion is not an issue, I think that circumcision should wait until a boy is old enough to make a considered decision for himself. Once a foreskin has been removed, you can't stick it back on again.

Whether your lover is circumcised or not, let's continue our up close and personal look at him . . . and now let's get *very* close.

Take his soft penis into your mouth and see if you can fit it all in. Biddie, 24, a fitness instructor from Cleveland, Ohio, said, "That's absolutely one of my favorite sexual kicks . . . taking a guy's cock into my mouth when it's soft, because you can swallow it all, and sometimes you can swallow one of his balls as well, although I've never managed two! Then what you do is, you suck it up against the roof of your mouth and you stick your tongue into the little hole, and hey presto! before you know it, it's starting to swell like bread rising. It's such an amazing feeling, right inside your mouth. It doesn't take long before you have to let his ball pop out, and then the rest of his cock, because it's, like, trebled in size, and it'll choke you."

Biddie also enjoyed sucking her lover's penis immediately after making love. "Of course it doesn't go up, but that means that you can chew it for longer. I mean, I really chew it like chewing gum, only not quite so hard. When you first take it into your mouth, it's so sexy, because it tastes of *his* sperm and your own pussy juice and if he's used a condom it tastes of rubber, too. Guys react differently. Some of them want you to leave them alone after sex. Some of them don't even want to *talk* to you, let alone have their cocks chewed. But most of them learn to love it . . . especially when they find that they get another hard-on much quicker than they've ever done before."

She was also an advocate of testicle sucking. "Guys love it, because girls hardly ever do it. They've heard so much about balls, how sensitive they are, and they're afraid they're going to hurt them. And it's like this bag of tricks, isn't it—this strange wrinkled bag with floaty slippery objects inside it. If you were going to design something to turn women on, you wouldn't actually come up with that, would you? But once you've learned how to suck a guy's balls, it's something really special. You can blow your boy-friend's mind, really. I did it to one guy and I turned him on so much he had to beg me to stop because he felt like he couldn't breathe."

So—now we've taken a look at how your lover's penis is constructed, let's take a look at his scrotum. I know—even the word "scrotum" is enough to put you off, isn't it? It's a name that was famously used for a butler in a comedy show, because he was a wrinkly old retainer.

Despite that, a man's scrotum contains the most important part of his sexual equipment—his testes, or testicles. The penis is just the delivery system. It is the testes that produce the male sex hormones which cause the changes that happen in a man's body when he reaches puberty—his beard, his deep-ening voice, and his ability to father children.

It is also the testes which produce sperm, and this is the reason they are suspended outside the main body cavity in a bag of skin. To produce sperm in sufficient quantities to guarantee that a man is capable of impregnating a woman, they need an ambient temperature of 95 degrees Fahrenheit, or 35 degrees Celsius, which is several degrees below normal body temperature.

Inside, your lover's scrotum is divided into two compartments, one containing each testis. The distinctive ridge on the outside will show you where this is, and if you rub the skin of his scrotum between finger and thumb you should be able to feel it, too. In almost all men, the left testis hangs slightly lower down than the right, but they can both be moved up and down by an arrangement of muscles. You can see these working for yourself. When it's very warm, the muscles relax and the testes hang low. When it's cold, they contract, and draw the testes closer to the body. If you want a really dramatic demonstration of this contraction, push your lover into a freezing-cold swimming pool.

If you (gently) take one of his testes in your fingertips, you will be able to fondle a miracle of science. Each testis is divided into two hundred and fifty compartments, and each compartment contains tiny, tightly coiled tubes, some eight hundred of them, each of them more than two feet long. These are his seminiferous tubules, and it is in these that sperm are being produced, tens of billions of them, every day.

The tubules join together and open out into a wider tube, which is coiled on top of each testis. You should be able to feel this, too. It's called the epididymis, which is Greek for "on top of the twins"—the "twins," of course, being your lover's balls.

Once they have been produced in the testes, new sperm are pushed up into the epididymis, where they spend about two weeks maturing. From here, they take a roundabout journey through the lower part of your partner's body along tubes called the vasa deferentia, into sperm storage areas called ampullae. The ampullae are close to the prostate gland, inside which the two spermatic cords join together and enter the urethra at the base of the penis.

The prostate gland lies just below the bladder and produces a number of chemicals, including prostaglandins. These are capable of inducing strong muscular contractions of the womb, and are thought to help the sperm to travel upward into your body. Prostaglandins have such a powerful effect on the womb that in a purified form they can actually bring on labor. Some advisers warn that pregnant women should avoid swallowing their lovers' semen, in case its prostaglandin content brings on early contractions, but you would probably have to drink it by the quart to be at any serious risk.

It's possible for you to feel your partner's prostate gland, and even to massage it. You can do this by lubricating your index finger and sliding it into his anus, as far as it will go. If you press your fingertip against the front wall of his rectum, you will feel his prostate as a spongy mass on the other side. You can massage it with a strong, rhythmic, beckoning motion. Most men find this intensely erotic, and it has been referred to as "the male G-spot." It can feel strange and unpleasant at first, but once he has grown used to it, a few minutes of intensive prostate massage can actually bring your lover to a climax, *without even touching his penis.*

"Whenever Rick says he doesn't feel like sex, I give him a finger-fuck up his ass and it always turns him on." That's Susan, 27, an insurance salesperson from Omaha, Nebraska. "He makes a show of stopping me, but not very hard, because I know how much he likes it. First of all I make my finger all slippery with face cream and then I push it into his asshole and start to rub him with this round-and-round motion. It almost always makes him hard, and sometimes it makes him come. Once or twice he's come without even getting hard: the sperm has just poured out of him all over the sheet."

Even many men are not aware that **erection** and **ejaculation** are quite separate processes. Ejaculation is caused by contraction of the pelvic muscles just behind the penis, and if a man is sexually stimulated enough (by having his prostate massaged, for instance, or by sexual fantasizing) it is quite possible for him to climax through a completely soft penis.

Some men consider that a climax produced by prostate massage is infinitely more erotic than a climax produced by stimulating the end of the penis. Perry, 36, a designer from St. Louis, Missouri, said, "It's a totally different experience. You're so out of yourself that you almost feel like you're taking a trip. At first it's uncomfortable, but gradually you get this real warm sensation . . . it's indescribable. It's like no climax you ever had before. The sperm flows out of your cock like a river, and you don't even have an erection."

So what does the prostate do? Along with various other glands just below it, it produces the fluid in which the sperm live and swim, and lubrication for the tip of the penis just before intercourse. You will have noticed that when your partner is sexually aroused, a drop or two of clear slippery liquid moistens his glans. It also prepares his urethra for the passage of sperm by neutralizing any chemicals in it which may harm them.

At the moment of climax, involuntary nerve signals cause a series of powerful muscular spasms. These shoot a mixture of sperm and seminal fluid into his urethra and out of the end of his penis. It is the seminal fluid that gives the sperm food and oxygen and triggers the tail-thrashing which propels them.

In case you've ever wondered about it—a muscular contraction makes sure that your lover's bladder is firmly closed off during his climax, both to prevent the sperm from going the wrong way and urine from being ejaculated. In fact men with a full erection find it extremely hard (if not impossible) to pee.

Once you've closely examined your partner's penis and testicles, try masturbating him so that he goes hard. Ask him to tell you exactly which grip he finds the most stimulating, and if there are any "extras" which he would enjoy, such as gently flicking his frenum (that thin stretch of skin just beneath his urethral opening) with your pinkie. Does he like it if you grip him very tight, or does he prefer it if you hold him more loosely? How far up the shaft of his penis does he prefer you to hold him? Does it turn him on if you dig your fingernails into his shaft? Does he want you to tug the skin of his scrotum—or claw that, too, to give him a little pain?

Ask him to show you how he holds himself when he masturbates. You can learn volumes about his sexual responses from that. In particular, watch the way he presses his thumb against his glans. Does he position it on top of the glans itself, or just behind the ridge? Does he use any kind of rippling motion with his fingers? Only he knows precisely what stimulates him the most, but if you're very observant you will learn to turn him on almost as well as he can.

As his climax approaches, he will be experiencing a tightening sensation deep between his legs, and a rising urgency to ejaculate. This is the time to keep a very close eye on the way that he is rubbing his penis, because you will probably see that his grip and his rhythm both change. Some men like to rub themselves fast and hard toward their climax, while others slow right down so that they can savor every last moment. Just before ejaculation, the pleasurable tension can be almost unbearable.

Watch as he actually shoots out his sperm. His rubbing will continue as he "milks" his penis. See how he does it, and how long he goes on doing it before his penis subsides. Some men like to fondle their penises for some minutes after their climax, while others lose all sexual interest almost immediately, and want to do nothing more than wipe up their semen and go on to do something else.

You can learn to stimulate his penis almost as well as he does . . . but you can learn to do something more. Because you won't be feeling the same urgency to ejaculate that he is, you can control his climax—delaying it, prolonging it, and even postponing it. This is how you can keep his erection up for much longer than he has ever been able to keep it up before, and how you can enjoy the benefits.

You should masturbate him manually as often as you can, and encourage him to do it in front of you, so that you can imitate his technique as closely as possible. Note that he won't always rub himself in exactly the same way. Depending on his mood, and the time available, he may masturbate extremely slowly or extremely fast. He may use a very different grip, and adjust his grip as he comes nearer and nearer to his climax.

Sheila, a 31-year-old interior designer from Oakland, California, said, "Gene used to be very shy when it came to discussing what he liked in bed. I'd rub his cock real slow and say, 'How do you like it when I do it like this?' and he'd say 'Great.' Then I'd rub it quick and say, 'Well, do you like it when I do it like *this*?' and he'd say 'Great.' I think he was amazed that a woman could be so interested in all the details of his sexual responses, you know? His mom and dad were both quite strict and religious, and his dad had told him that boys who touch their private parts for any other reason except washing them or taking a whiz were all condemned to go to hell. As if his dad never spanked the monkey when *he* was a boy. As if every single man on the planet hasn't done it, at least once.

"It took a while for Gene to show me the particular ways he liked to have his cock fondled. When we were lying in bed, I used to reach over and play with his cock and his balls, even if I wasn't looking to make love . . . even if we were only watching a movie on TV, or maybe we'd already made love when we first went to bed. To begin with, I think it made him feel a little uncomfortable. He didn't quite know how to react, because he'd never had a girlfriend who wanted to fondle him as often as I did. Like, once it's all over, most girls don't carry on playing with their lovers' cocks, but I love squishing Gene's cock and his balls in my hand when he's all sticky with sperm and juice. Sucking him, too. I guess my attitude is that when you're having a relationship, your bodies belong to each other. That means that Gene's cock belongs to me just as much as my pussy belongs to him. If he starts to play with my clitoris in the middle of the night, I'm not going to complain—in fact I wish he'd do it more often.

"Once Gene had gotten used to the idea of my touching him so much, he began to loosen up, and soon he was telling me . . . you know, a little harder please, Sheila, or a little faster, or a little further up. After that, I didn't have any problems in getting him to show me how he jerked himself off. I would say to every woman everywhere: get your guy to show you how he jerks himself off. It's fascinating. And educational, too. And of course every man does it different, because they don't have monkey-spanking classes in grade school.

"Three things I noticed in particular about the way in which Gene jerks off. He will start off holding his cock quite loosely, with his thumb pressing lightly on the upper side of it, just below the bump [the corona]. His fingers play up and down the underside, almost like he's playing the flute. He strokes himself with the tip of his index finger, just below the opening in his cock. Now and then, his pinkie comes down and gently tickles the dividing line in the middle of his balls.

"After a while he starts gripping his cock much tighter, and pumping on it harder. I guess you'd describe it as a pull-down motion, like he's a plumber trying to clear a blocked-up drain with a sink plunger. His thumb moves up until it's pressing directly on the head of his cock, and he's squeezing it pretty hard.

"You can tell that he's coming close to his climax, because he starts holding his breath, and his chest starts to flush red. I can always tell when he's just about to shoot, because he suddenly stops gripping his cock so hard, and his pumping slows down until it's one . . . and . . . *two* . . . and . . . one . . . and . . . *two* . . . because his sperm's already on the way and he knows there's nothing he can do to stop it and he wants to enjoy every last second of it. At least, that's the way he described it to me. He says he has this wonderful tingling sensation right between his legs, and he can actually feel the sperm rising in his cock before it comes shooting out.

"When he actually climaxes, he tends to pull his cock two or three times outwards, like he's stretching it, and then he pulls it back again. After that, he relaxes, but I've noticed that he goes on massaging his cock and his balls, using his sperm as a lubricant. I think that's very important . . . just like women like to be cuddled after sex, men like to have their cocks played with. They seem to find it very relaxing and reassuring . . . like, it's good for them to feel that you didn't find them sexually attractive just because their cocks were sticking up.

"I have absolutely no inhibitions whatsoever about asking Gene to jerk off in front of me, and to show me what he likes best. How else am I supposed to know? And why should we go on day after day pretending that I'm rubbing his cock just the way he likes it best, when I'm not. I've diddled myself in front of him, too, so that he can see how I like to have my clitoris fingered. I told this to one of my girlfriends and she was shocked. But as far as I'm concerned, an intimate relationship is an intimate relationship, and that means you don't hide anything. That doesn't mean we don't have privacy. I don't want Gene in the toilet with me, but then I don't suppose *he* wants to be there, either.

"But when it comes to sexual sensations, when your partner only has to move his finger a sixteenth of an inch to make the difference between 'Mmm' and 'Wow!' . . . what's wrong with telling him? In my opinion, you only live your life once . . . why not enjoy it while you can?"

Sheila's description of a "pulling-down" motion is very vivid: most men find it very arousing if the outer skin of their penis is pulled down toward the base of their penis, sometimes quite hard. This has the effect of stretching the frenum and the area directly behind the corona, which is particularly sensitive to licking and gentle stroking with the fingertips.

You can treat your lover's penis quite robustly. You will see by the way in which he masturbates that the slang terms "bashing the bishop" or "beating the meat" are fairly accurate descriptions of the ways in which men manhandle themselves. You can grip his penis very tightly, and you can rub it hard, but you should avoid any wild, abrupt, jerking movements, especially at awkward angles, because these can accidentally tear the fibers of his penis, or at the very least cause him a great deal of pain.

As we saw in the question-and-answer section earlier in this book, you can actually "fracture" a man's penis if you put your full weight on it when it's erect (not if it's inside your vagina, of course, but if you sit on it with your thigh or buttock, or violently pull it downward between his legs, against the normal angle of erection).

One of the most important things to watch for when your lover shows you how he masturbates is "the point of no return"—that is, the moment when his involuntary muscular contractions begin, and he can't stop himself from ejaculating. The best way of telling when he's just about to climax is for him to shout out, "I'm coming!" But if he prefers to keep silent when he masturbates, as some men do, ask him to squeeze your hand instead. Look at him carefully. Every muscle in his body will be tense. His scrotum will be tightly wrinkled, so that his testicles will look like walnuts. His feet will begin to curl. His face will look flushed and he will hold his breath for long periods, in between gasps, so that he can concentrate all of his physical feeling between his legs. He may be gritting his teeth.

The first few times that he masturbates for you, you can allow him to ejaculate. Then—the next time he does it—ask him if he can manage to stop himself, just before it's too late. He may find this difficult. He will probably find it extremely frustrating. But this is the key to keeping your man up all night, and once he has become accustomed to the idea of not necessarily reaching a climax when he is sexually stimulated, he will discover (as you will) that there are some amazing sexual experiences just waiting for your mutual pleasure.

As I mentioned in the foreword to this book, the Western male's idea of sexual intercourse is very much climax-driven. No climax, no satisfaction. In fact, most men think that if they haven't reached a climax, it hardly counts as having sex at all. The male climax is especially glorified in pornography—with pictures of men ejaculating over women's faces and breasts. Probably the most extreme example of this is *bukakke,* which admittedly had its origins in Japan but which is now an Internet favorite in the United States and Europe. Young girls are masturbated on by dozens and sometimes scores of men, until their faces look like cakes covered in white frosting. Some girls gag down pints of semen from glass flasks, or have it poured over their heads.

Jim, 29, an architect from Seattle, Washington, said, "Releasing your sexual tension—I mean, that's the whole point of going to bed with a girl, isn't it? The only times I haven't managed to come is when I've been too drunk and I've fallen asleep halfway through it."

Men who think like Jim often complain that if they *don't* reach a climax, they will suffer from that mysterious mythical ailment known as "blue balls."

Kim, 19, a hairstylist from Charleston, South Carolina, said, "The first time I ever had sex with a boy was not because I really wanted to, but because he told me that he had 'blue balls,' and that if he didn't have a climax then it was going to ruin his chances of ever being a father. His parents were away and we'd been kissing and fondling each other all evening. I let him take off my bra and play with my nipples and then I let him put his hand inside my panties, but I got scared then because I'd never let a boy do that before, and I didn't want to have intercourse with him. But he zipped open his pants and showed me his cock and his balls, and he said we had to have sex because I'd given him blue balls, and he could be damaged for life. He made out like it was my fault for teasing him so much, and like it was my responsibility to make sure he had a climax. So what could I do? I let him have sex with me. At least I had the brains to make sure that he wore a rubber. It wasn't a good experience. I was worried that I had really hurt him, and so I couldn't let myself go and enjoy it, and in any case he came to a climax almost as soon as he put himself inside me. So he wasn't the greatest lover that a girl could hope for. And now what? You're telling me that 'blue balls' is just a scam?''

Keith, 24, a law student from Indianapolis, Indiana, asserted, ''If a guy gets sexually aroused, then it's essential that he goes all the way to a climax. It's not just a psychological thing, it's a physical imperative. If you get really turned on and then you don't ejaculate, it's bad for you. Your balls turn blue, you get blocked tubes, and it can make you sterile.''

I'll bet that's what Keith tells all his girlfriends. The notorious ''blue balls'' excuse has been used by men for countless generations to persuade girls to have sex, or at least into ''getting them off'' by oral sex or masturbation.

The truth is that when a man has been making out with a girl without sexual release, he may notice a bluish tinge to his testicles. During sexual arousal, as we have seen, more blood flows into a man's sexual organs than flows out of them (hence a blood-filled erection). If sexual arousal continues for some time without a climax, the genital area remains engorged with blood, which *may* cause aching and a feeling of discomfort.

But it's not really his balls that turn blue. It's the skin of his scrotum, which in any case is naturally darker than his penis. When he's aroused, blood doesn't flow only into the penis to make it stiff, it fills the surrounding area, too—just as your vaginal area flushes a rosy color when you're excited.

The longer the blood remains in his genital area, the more oxygen it gives up, and the darker it appears. So what does he get? Blue (or at least maroon-colored) balls. But don't worry, they aren't going to wither away from lack of oxygen and drop off—there is still plenty of fresh, bright blood circulating in his scrotum.

Men who give you the "blue balls" excuse are right about one thing: a climax *will* release the congestion and return his scrotum to its normal everyday color. But that doesn't mean that you have to provide that climax—either by having intercourse, or giving him oral sex, or rubbing him by hand. He's a big boy, and he's perfectly capable of giving himself a climax, if you don't feel like doing it.

"Blue balls" aren't harmful. They don't affect a man's virility or his fertility in any way. Even without a climax, his scrotum will gradually lose its blue hue, and the ache will die away. (Incidentally . . . not all men suffer "blue balls" when they are sexually aroused, so if your partner's scrotum *doesn't* go darker when you play with his penis, that doesn't mean that you're not turning him on.)

Many women also think that the sexual act isn't complete unless their partner reaches a climax, and that if he doesn't, they have somehow failed to give him the satisfaction he expects, and is entitled to.

However—if you want your lover to have stronger and longer-lasting erections, so that you can both enjoy hours of sensational lovemaking—then you have to start thinking about his climax in a completely different way.

Orgasm is important for women, too, but when a woman climaxes, that doesn't automatically mean that intercourse is over—as it does when a man ejaculates, and his penis starts to subside. After your orgasm, you can carry on making love, and experience further orgasms almost immediately afterward. A man not only loses his erection, but he loses interest in having sex—sometimes, quite dramatically.

"Once I've come, I just want to be left alone," said Newton, a 26-year-old IT salesman from Baltimore, Maryland. "The girl I'm with can be the most beautiful girl you've ever seen, but all I want to do is rest and think. I don't want to talk and I don't like to be fiddled with, especially my cock. After I've had a climax I have to force myself to give a girl a kiss and a cuddle and tell her how gorgeous she is. I only do that because I don't want her to think that I'm only after her body. I know it sounds bad, but that's just the way I feel."

The instant sexual turnoff that Newton feels after his climax is extremely common. "I couldn't believe it," said Andrea, 25, a teacher from Philadelphia, Pennsylvania. "One minute John couldn't get enough of me . . . I really thought he was going to eat me alive. The next minute he didn't even want me to *touch* him. He couldn't even bear it when I breathed in his ear."

The way in which men's sexual desire disappears down the plughole after they have climaxed leaves many women bewildered and unsatisfied, especially if they were expecting hours of erotic shenanigans. In so many cases, women have been promised "a night of passion" but the reality turns out to be three or four minutes of grunting, followed by premature ejaculation, a kiss on the top of the head, and seven hours of snoring.

But you can learn to control your partner's penis, and teach *him* how to control it, too, particularly when he climaxes—that's if he climaxes at all. If you do, your whole sex life will blossom like a garden full of roses. You will discover sensations that you haven't even fantasized about, because you didn't know that they were possible . . . and so will he.

Your partner gets an erection for a variety of reasons, some of them physical and some of them psychological. The whole process is really quite complicated, and it's easy to understand how something quite minor (such as worrying about an unpaid bill) can affect a man's potency.

Your partner is sexually aroused either:

(a) By touching you and smelling you.
(b) By looking at you.
(c) By the imminent prospect of making love to you.
(d) By sexual fantasies.
(e) By you touching him.
(f) By you acting flirtatiously.
(g) By you talking dirty.
(h) By any combination of any of these stimuli.

When he is excited, chemicals are released into his nervous system which cause the blood vessels in his penis to open up, so that the blood flows in and his penis becomes erect. At the same time, he is gripped by the almost irresistible urge to penetrate your vagina with his penis, and to move himself in and out of you until he ejaculates.

But with practice, you can help him to control this urge. Together, you can learn techniques which will give him all the pleasure of building up to a climax, and then the new pleasure of delaying it. In time, he should be able to maintain an erection literally for hours, while you can satisfy yourself with it in any way that takes your fancy.

I'm not suggesting that you try to make love like this every night. Once or twice a week is probably enough for most lovers, no matter how highly sexed they are. After all, most of us have jobs to go to in the morning, and one of the essentials for all-night sex is not having any anxieties about staying awake until the sun peeps over the windowsill.

Now that you have watched your lover masturbating himself until he has almost reached a climax, but then stopped himself, see if you can do it for him. You need to practice this as often as you can, until you have the confidence to take him right to the very edge of ejaculation, and then stop him. The first few times you try it, you will need to ask him to give you a running commentary on how he is feeling . . . even if he just says "That's nice" or "Slower."

You will also need to decide on a prearranged signal so that he can indicate to you the precise moment when the tension between his legs is approaching the point of no return, and that he is just about to ejaculate. Maybe he can say something like "That's it!" or "Coming!" but many couples prefer a silent method of communication. It's more intimate, and it's instantaneous. The favorite is for the man gently but firmly to pinch his partner's earlobe between finger and thumb.

At this point, you will have to find the most effective and the least frustrating way of preventing your lover from climaxing (wouldn't want him to get "blue balls," would we?). One way of doing this is to use the "squeeze technique." Enthusiastically promoted by Masters and Johnson, the "squeeze technique" has been used with notable success as a treatment for premature ejaculation. A man is usually diagnosed as suffering from premature ejaculation if he climaxes within thirty seconds or less of having inserted his penis into his partner. Personally, I prefer to define it as climaxing before he really wants to— in other words, if he doesn't have total control over the moment when he ejaculates, and feels that he is always finishing too soon.

The "squeeze technique" is one of the simple but practical ways in which you can help your lover to regain mastery over his own erection. When you're making love, he should take his penis out of you as soon as he feels that he's coming close to his climax. This in itself will be the signal for you to act.

All you have to do is grip his penis with your thumb pressed against the upper side, on the ridge of his glans, and your index finger and your middle finger pressed against the underside, against the opening. Squeeze quite hard, counting slowly to five, or until your partner indicates that the urge to ejaculate has subsided.

He may experience a softening of his erection after a squeeze, but you will almost always find that you can arouse him again by rubbing him with your hand, or by manipulating his glans upward and downward between the moistened lips of your vulva.

You can use the "squeeze technique" again and again before he finally climaxes. Not only will you be doing yourself a favor by making your lovemaking last much longer, you will be helping your partner to gain complete control over his sexual responses.

The squeeze can dramatically improve your sex life even if your partner *isn't* suffering from premature ejaculation. Here's how it made all the difference to Helen, a 32-year-old Realtor from Napa, California.

"I always thought our lovemaking was pretty good. Neil could last a good half hour, sometimes longer. We used to try all sorts of positions and make love in all different places—like the kitchen, or the hallway, or the backseat of the car when it was parked in the garage. Once we went to my parents' house and he made love to me standing up in the glasshouse with my skirt around my waist, when we were supposed to be picking fresh tomatoes for lunch.

"The only trouble was, I very rarely reached orgasm. Not during intercourse, anyhow. Almost every time we made love, I could feel the first stirrings of it, if you understand what I mean, and a few times I was very, very close. If I didn't reach orgasm, Neil always made sure that he satisfied me using his fingers or his tongue, and that was good. I mean he was very considerate, sexually as well as every other way. But I still felt this deep-seated need to have an orgasm while he was actually inside me."

Women are sexually aroused much more slowly than men, and one of the commonest sexual problems is caused by men climaxing before their partners are even halfway toward achieving an orgasm. Research into orgasmic response has shown that the time it takes for a woman to climax may be strongly affected by her upbringing, her previous sexual experiences, and her general feeling of well-being and security. Women who don't relax during intercourse usually find that it takes longer for them to reach an orgasm—and, just like men, their climax can be delayed by mentally detaching themselves from their lovemaking.

This is why it is so important for your lover to keep his erection for as long as possible. After I had talked to Helen, I advised her to try the "squeeze technique." Even though Neil didn't suffer from premature ejaculation in the sense that he climaxed in less than thirty seconds after inserting his penis into her vagina, he was still coming too soon for Helen to experience the kind of orgasm she really craved. I also advised her that—when it came to making love—she should try to initiate the kind of play that stimulated *her*, rather than worry about him.

"Neil wasn't too enthusiastic about it, to begin with. I think he believed that it was casting aspersions on his manhood. But he seemed to feel better about it when I said that it wasn't him who was climaxing too quick, it was me who was climaxing too slow. We tried it for the first time when we went to spend the weekend at my friend Laura's house in Sonoma. We'd had a great evening with lots of good food and wine, and the bedroom was very romantic, with a four-poster bed made of pine, with a Navajo throw.

"I did a striptease routine for Neil, dancing around the bedroom and never quite letting him touch me. Then I pushed him back onto the bed and unbuttoned his shirt and his pants. I undressed him, kissing him and biting his nipples, because I know he likes that. When I pulled off his pants and his shorts, he tried to take control, like he usually does, but I wouldn't let him. It had to be me who was in charge of what was going on, right from the very beginning.

"When he was naked, I took the pins out of my hair, so that it fell down over my shoulders and my breasts. I still have very long hair but it was even longer then. I swung my head from side to side so that my hair brushed across his cock and his balls, and he was standing up so hard that his cock was actually throbbing with his heartbeat.

"I looped my hair around his cock, just underneath the knob, and I pulled it so tight that his knob swelled and went purple. Like you told me, I was doing all the things that I wanted to do . . . the things that turned me on. I don't know whether I'm a secret Madam Whiplash, but hurting a man does excite me. I bit his knob and I clawed his balls with my fingernails, so that they bled.

"Then I shifted myself up the bed a little and sat astride his face. I had never acted so dominant in bed before, and I think it made him feel kind of uneasy, but his cock was still sticking up like a big red rocket, so it was obvious that it turned him on, too. I put my hand behind his head and lifted it off the bed so that his face was pressed right into my pussy. He licked me and sucked my lips and by that time I was so wet that his face was covered in juice.

"I moved back down so that I could take hold of his cock and guide it into my pussy. It felt fantastic, sliding all the way in, right up to his balls, until his knob touched my womb and made me jump. I went up and down on him very slow, very rhythmic, just like you said, and I closed my eyes so that I could think about this amazing feeling between my legs, this huge cock right up inside me as far as it could possibly go.

"Neil started to make little 'unh' noises, which he always did just before he climaxed. I went up and down on him two or three more times, and then he suddenly said, 'Now, now, it's almost there!' I took his cock out of me and squeezed it the way you showed me, hard, between my thumb and my fingers. I counted slowly up to five, and then he smiled at me and said, 'That's it, that's fine.'

"His cock had softened a little, but I leaned forward and took it into my mouth, and sucked it. I stared at him all the time I was doing it, right into his eyes. Men love you staring at them while you suck their cocks. It's like you're saying, 'I'll do anything for you, O master,' but at the same time it's like saying, 'If I wanted to, I could bite your cock off.' It's like being submissive and dominant, both at the same time.

"Neil's cock soon went hard again, and I slipped it back into my pussy. We made love like this for nearly three hours. Maybe it was longer. I took his cock out and squeezed it maybe six or seven times, to stop him from having a climax, and after a while he seemed to find it easier to hold back.

"I had my first orgasm after about forty-five minutes. I could feel it coming . . . I could feel it gradually tightening up inside me like somebody twisting a rubber band tighter and tighter and tighter and there was absolutely nothing I could do to stop it. I sat still with Neil's cock right up inside me and I literally quaked, because the feeling was so incredible. Neil said afterward that he could feel my pussy rippling against his cock, and that he had bitten his cheek to stop himself from climaxing, too.

"I finally masturbated Neil to a climax about three-thirty in the morning, when I had reached orgasm at least five times, and we were both exhausted. I lay next to him and rubbed his cock and suddenly the sperm shot out of it like a geyser, all over my hand and my stomach and my breasts. Neil massaged it all over me until it dried up. That's another thing that really turns men on—shooting their sperm all over you. For Neil, I think that was a way of showing his potency. I didn't mind. In fact, it turned me on, too. Don't ask me to explain why people do things like that when they make love. If it turns you on, do it, that's what I say—do it and enjoy it. I used to have a boyfriend who liked to shoot his sperm all over my feet.

"Laura and Mike gave us a very strange look the next morning. I think we'd kept them awake all night with our shouting and panting and bed-squeaking. They must have thought we were sex maniacs."

Helen clearly identified the problem in her sex life—the arousal gap between herself and Neil—and made an effort to fix it. The solution was extremely simple, but it can take courage to tell your partner that something isn't quite right between you. In fact, that's probably the hardest part, because when it comes to sex, we are all highly sensitive about our performance, especially men. The last thing you want to do is explain to your partner why you're not sexually satisfied, only to find that your criticism leads to him losing his erection.

In the next chapter, we'll see how you can form a friendship with your partner's penis, and how this can make it very much easier for you to tell him what you really want in bed.

Two: Penis Pal

Making Friends with Your Partner's Parts

When you first meet a man you find sexually attractive, you are actually meeting two separate individuals: the penis, and the other bit.

Because very few women fully understand how independent-minded their partner's penises are, they can be mystified by any failing in their partner's performance. "His mouth says he loves me but his penis says he doesn't."

They simply don't realize that when you enter into an intimate liaison with a man, it is invariably a ménage à trois—you, the man, and the man's penis—and that more often or not, the penis is in charge, no matter what the man has to say about it.

It is no exaggeration to say that thousands of unhappy sexual relationships could be saved every year if women understood more about the remarkable relationship between men and their penises. As I have mentioned earlier, even many sexually experienced women fail fully to grasp that a man's penis has a mind of its own, and that its owner cannot *wish* it into going hard, or deliberately make it hard by flexing his pelvic muscles, or any other natural means. He can take hold of it and masturbate it with his hand, but even then it may very well refuse to stand up and pay attention.

A man can deliberately turn his mind to sexual fantasies, or look at pornographic magazines or videos, and it is very possible that his penis will rise. But if it doesn't—or if it gets hard and quickly softens again—there is very little he can do about it.

(On the other hand, if his penis is already hard, he may very well be able to think it into going *soft*, particularly if he makes an effort to turn his mind to something else apart from sex. But apart from that he has almost no mental or physical control over his erections whatsoever.)

Jeannette, 34, an accountant from Detroit, Michigan, said that she always "kind of" believed that men could produce an erection to order, although she wasn't 100 percent clear about it. For this reason she was devastated when her husband Duane began to suffer from problems at bedtime.

"I wouldn't say I was ignorant about sex. More like *vague*. You ask most women how their partner's dick gets stiff and they simply don't know—not exactly. Maybe they'll tell you 'He just feels like the wild thing and up it goes.' I used to think that if a man goes without sex for a week or two, he builds up so much come [semen] inside of him that he's just got to let it out. I think one of my boyfriends told me that, so that I would give him a hand job.

"I guess I always knew that men's dicks go stiff

even when they don't want them to. I've seen a few boys getting real embarrassed when they had a hard-on in their shorts. But I also thought that when they felt like making love they could make them go stiff on purpose, same as making their biceps bulge."

Duane—who is also an accountant—had a crisis at work. His company's auditors discovered a "black hole" in their annual budget, and Duane was one of six employees under suspicion. "They weren't saying that he was guilty of embezzlement, but they were trying to make out that he had made some major miscalculations. He kept reassuring me that everything was fine, but I was beginning to wonder if he was telling me the truth. He's very proud about his work, very particular."

One of the results of Duane's anxiety was an inability to achieve a full erection. "It happened for the first time one Thursday night, after he'd been called up in front of the board. I thought that I'd really relax him that night, take his mind off his worries, give him a good time. I made him his favorite dinner and then we took our wine and went to bed. But he couldn't do it. His dick went *bigger*, you know, but it didn't get hard enough to get inside me. It flopped this way and that way but I couldn't get it in. I tried sucking it and licking it, and then rubbing it, but it just got smaller and smaller, and in the end I had to give it up.

"I was disappointed, for sure, but I didn't think it was the end of the world. I just imagined that Duane was tired. But when I tried again on Saturday morning, which is our usual time for making love, he couldn't get any kind of a hard-on at all.

"Again, I thought, 'He's too tired, never mind, he's had a very difficult week.' But the same thing happened on Sunday, and every night the week after. He didn't say anything but when he went to bed he turned his back on me and I began to get the feeling that he didn't even like me to touch him."

Jeannette could readily accept that physical tiredness was a reason for Duane not to get an erection, but she couldn't really understand how problems at the office could affect him so dramatically. On the contrary, she thought that sex would help to take his mind off things. Since she believed that he was able to exert some physical control over his erections—in other words, that he could make his penis go hard just by willing it to—she quickly came to assume that he was losing interest in her. She even began to suspect that he might be having an affair with a female colleague at work. "I thought that maybe the crisis in the office had brought them closer together, because they were both involved with the same investigation."

It is alarming how quickly erectile dysfunction can break down the mutual trust between a man and a woman. Sometimes it can take as few as three or four failed erections before a relationship is seriously damaged by humiliation on one side and suspicion on the other. And once trust has broken down, building it up again can be a long and very painful process.

As I mentioned in the foreword, you need to take action immediately. If a wide crack appeared in your living-room ceiling, you wouldn't just paper it over, or pretend that it wasn't there. So why hesitate when a similar crack appears in your sexual relationship?

What Duane should have done. Right from his very first failure to achieve an erection, Duane should have reassured Jeannette that he *wanted* to make love to her, but that the pressures he was having to face at work were making it difficult for his brain to "let go." He should have explained that she still turned him on, but his work problem kept nagging in the back of his mind and made it difficult for him to concentrate on making love.

Without being a mind reader, Duane couldn't have known that Jeannette didn't fully understand all the complicated factors that cause an erection, and that she was beginning to wonder if he didn't find her sexually attractive any more. It was very likely that Duane himself didn't fully understand how many chemical, psychological and sensory stimuli were responsible for making his penis go hard.

But even though his penis hadn't gone fully erect, he shouldn't have stopped holding her close and kissing and caressing her. It was important for him to show her that he still found her sexually arousing. Not only that, he needed to demonstrate that he didn't feel like a failure, and that his sexual confidence in himself was undented.

At the same time as cuddling her, he should have told her that he would have loved to have an erection, but because he couldn't give it his undivided attention, his penis was sulking. It might sound a simplistic way of putting it, but if a man's mind and body aren't in good working order, his penis can refuse to respond to almost any kind of stimulation, mental or physical. The late British historian and notorious womanizer, Alan Clarke, once went through a period of impotence and said it was like having empty trousers.

The worst thing that Duane could have done was turn his back on Jeannette in bed and worry in silence about his failure to get an erection. He had enough problems on his plate without impotence, too. He needed to enlist Jeannette's help, but Jeannette could only help him if she knew what was wrong.

I'm not saying that it's easy for a man to talk to his partner about his erection difficulties. After all, an erect penis is what makes a man feel like a man. But penis problems are almost always too complicated to sort out single-handed, even if they're not especially serious or long-lasting. Almost every man has experienced ED at one time or another, and there is absolutely no shame in his admitting to his partner that he is having trouble in getting his penis to stand up. In fact it shows that he's keen to sort out his problem as soon as possible and get back to sex the way it was . . . or even better.

The longer Duane suffered his ED in silence, the more difficult it was going to be for him to regain his potency and his sexual self-respect.

What Jeannette should have done. From the earliest days of her getting together with Duane, Jeannette should have formed her own special relationship with Duane's penis. That means that she should have learned its basic physiology (as explained in Chapter One) and how and why it went up and down. If she had done that, she would never have been under the illusion that Duane was capable of achieving an erection just by thinking, "I know! I'll have an erection!" *Bingggg!!* On the very first night that he failed to get an erection, she would have suspected that his problems at work were causing him much more stress than he was telling her.

Jeannette should have made the intimate acquaintance of Duane's penis by joining it in the shower, or in the bathtub. It would have been undressed already, and it would have been a natural thing for her to take hold of it and soap it. Washing his penis would have given her plenty of time to feel his shaft and his glans, and to explore the mysteries of his scrotum. She could have probed her finger up his anus, too, and seen how much Duane enjoyed *that*.

By fondling his penis in the shower, she should have been able to establish some degree of "ownership" over it. She should have massaged it with plenty of shower gel until it stiffened, and if Duane tried to pull it away, she should have made sure that she held onto it. She should have talked to it, as if it were a separate person. "How do you like it when I rub you like that, Fido?" (or whatever pet name she decided to call it.) She should have kneeled down in the shower and sucked it, talking to it from time to time.

During the course of her relationship with Duane,

she should have taken every opportunity to become more intimate with his penis. If he was sprawled on the couch watching TV, she should have opened his pants, taken out his penis, and treated it to a fondle or a suck. "*He* likes it, even if *you* don't." If Duane was asleep in bed in the morning, she should have played with his penis and his balls to see if she could make his penis stiff.

This sounds lighthearted, but it really works. It enables you to establish a high degree of control over your partner's autonomic nervous system, and can give you the power to make his penis erect even when he doesn't want it to be, or when he is suffering from stress or worry or some other inhibiting factor.

The trouble is, very few women take the time to get to know their partner's penis as well as they should, or even know that they ought to. Ask yourself these ten questions, *honestly*, and see how diligent you have been at making friends with Fido.

1) I often play with my partner's penis when it is soft. AGREE/DISAGREE

2) I hardly ever fondle my partner's testicles. AGREE/DISAGREE

3) I usually carry on playing with my partner's penis after we have finished having intercourse. AGREE/DISAGREE

4) I am reluctant to take my partner's penis into my mouth. AGREE/DISAGREE

5) I like to fondle my partner's penis even if we're not in the bedroom. AGREE/DISAGREE

6) I have never masturbated my partner's penis to a climax. AGREE/DISAGREE

7) I would not be shy about gripping my partner's penis really hard. AGREE/DISAGREE

8) I don't know how long my partner's penis is when it's erect. AGREE/DISAGREE

9) I like the taste and smell of my partner's semen. AGREE/DISAGREE

10) I could not recognize my partner by his genitals alone. AGREE/DISAGREE

If you answered "AGREE" to more odd-numbered questions than even-numbered questions, then you have already started to develop a very close understanding with your partner's penis, and the chances are that you're both going to be very happy together.

If you answered "AGREE" to more even-numbered questions than odd-numbered questions, then you really need to work harder at your relationship with your partner's penis before it starts to feel neglected.

Jeannette should have made sure that she was at least reasonably knowledgeable about the way in which Duane's penis worked. If she had done this, she should have had the self-assurance to fondle it and massage it when it was soft with just as much passion as she did when it was erect. A woman who can do this is the kind of woman who can win a man's sexual confidence for life.

While *gently* continuing to fondle his flaccid penis Jeannette should have asked Duane if there was anything worrying him. His work? His tax returns? She could have made up a story about a friend of hers whose husband lost his job and also lost his erections for a while, but who is now firing on all cylinders. There is no harm in a little white lie like that, especially if it serves to show your partner how sexually understanding you are, and helps to restore his self-respect.

However, there are some questions which she specifically should NOT have asked him. "You do still love me, don't you?" And, "I do still turn you on?" Questions like these have the effect of blaming *him* for his failure to get an erection, whereas he needed to be reassured that the cause of his temporary impotence was entirely external. More than anything else, Duane needed to know that Jeannette still regarded him as virile, and that he was still capable of showing her that he loved her, even if he was suffering from a temporary case of the flops.

Of course there will always be times when a man *does* fall out of love with a woman, and no longer finds her sexually exciting, but that is a different problem altogether, and no amount of reassurance can fix it. In Duane and Jeannette's case, there was nothing basically wrong with their sexual relationship . . . it was only Fido who was letting his side down.

If Duane had immediately told Jeannette that he still found her as sexy as ever, and that it was worry at work that was causing his erection problems—or if Jeannette had immediately asked Duane what was bothering him—they could have started to sort out his ED from the very first time it happened.

Jeannette should have told him:

(a) that she understood why he couldn't get an erection, but

(b) that she wasn't going to allow some stupid crisis at the office to ruin their sex life, and so

(c) they were going to carry on making love as usual, whether his penis got hard or not, and enjoy it just as much as ever.

At the same time, she should have made up her mind that she was going to do everything necessary to shake his penis out of its sulks. This would mean getting to know how it worked and how it responded to different kinds of stimulation, and performing some sexual acts that maybe she had never thought about trying before.

It was vital for Jeannette to have a positive attitude. Although erection failure is nothing to joke about, she should have tried to be good-humored, and treated it just as a sexual hiccup. In almost all cases of psychogenic impotence, if you *treat* it like a hiccup, it doesn't have to amount to anything more.

If it persists, then you obviously will need more help, but you should still remain upbeat about it. These days, there are plenty of ways in which ED can be quickly and effectively overcome—and sometimes just *knowing* this helps a man to get over his problems.

As we have seen, the shower or the bathtub are natural locations for striking up an intimate acquaintance with your partner's penis. But wherever you are, you shouldn't miss an opportunity to get to know it better.

Oral sex, or **fellatio,** is one of the best ways to develop a close relationship with your partner's penis. Your tongue and your lips and your mouth are highly sensitive, and as you lick and suck his penis you should be able to sense its responses in detail. Does it become stiffer when you probe the tip of your tongue into its urethra? Can you bring it to a climax if you simply "fuck" it with your mouth relaxed?

During oral sex, you are face-to-face with his penis, and don't forget that *you* are in charge. That means you can play with his penis in any way you like for as long as you like. Having said that, however, a considerable percentage of women are reticent about giving their partners oral sex, not so much because they don't want to, but because they are unsure of exactly what to do, and are concerned that they might somehow "do it wrong." Men are always desperate to give the impression that they are highly experienced lovers, but women are just as worried about appearing amateurish in bed as they are.

Kirsty, 24, a teacher from Watertown, Massachusetts, said that her closest friend Liz was always telling her that the way to a man's heart was through oral sex, but whenever she tried it herself she was never sure that she was giving her partners what they really wanted. "Most of them simply lie there or sit there and say nothing. I can't tell if they're enjoying it or not, or whether they're looking at their watches and wondering when I'm going to stop. Sometimes they run their hands into my hair, and once or twice they'll say something like, 'Oh, baby . . . that feels so good.' But apart from that, I have no idea if I'm doing it right."

Usually, Kirsty used to stop giving her partners oral sex after only a few minutes "because I was sure that it wasn't going anyplace, and that I was *never* going to bring them to a climax."

You have to remember that oral sex is a little bit of sexual theater. It's a way of showing your partner that he turns you on so much that you could eat him. Women who are good at oral sex are very aware of this, and will excite their lover's eyes as much as his penis. In reality, licking and sucking his penis—while highly enjoyable—is not usually the quickest way of bringing a man to a climax. Kirsty felt that she wasn't getting very far with her fellatio because she didn't realize that most of her partners needed rather more vigorous stimulation than she could give them with lips and tongue alone. Take a look at any oral sex scene in a pornographic video and you will see that as the girls bring the men closer to ejaculation, they are not only sucking their penises but rubbing them furiously with their fists.

You *can* bring a man to a climax by oral stimulation alone, but it will probably take you a lot longer than a combination of sucking and licking and manual masturbation—so if that's what you feel like doing, don't lose your nerve and give up. Your partner may *appear* to be unresponsive, but more than likely he's concentrating very hard on the feelings that you're giving him, both physically and mentally, and loving every second of it. Think of the way that *you* respond when your partner arouses you with his tongue: tense, muscles rigid, your mind focused on nothing but the growing sensation of pleasure between your legs. It isn't easy to show your appreciation at a time like this, no matter how much you're enjoying it.

On the other hand, don't forget that you're training your lover's penis to get stiffer quicker and to stay stiffer for longer, so bringing him to a climax isn't the be-all and end-all. In fact, the longer you can delay it, the better. It's the pleasure you give him that counts, and the enjoyment which *you* derive from it, too. Oral sex is a very good way of postponing your lover's climax, because you can easily slow things down by sucking less vigorously or licking more delicately, while still giving him a highly erotic display of sexual stimulation.

Tessa is a 29-year-old club hostess from Atlantic City, New Jersey, and she admits to having had "fifty or sixty lovers, maybe more." She said that she likes oral sex because it gives her absolute control over the pace and style of her sexual encounters. "I've never met a single man who doesn't love it, but none of them realize that I'm taking charge."

She explained that when she takes a man back to her apartment for sex, she slows the situation down by putting on mood music and pouring him a glass of wine. "Most men want to tear your clothes off and jump right into bed, but where's the enjoyment in that? It's all over in three and a half minutes, and what are you going to do for the rest of the night?

You're going to have to wait for at least a half hour before there's any chance of another erection—that's if he hasn't dropped off to sleep."

Tessa usually takes the initiative by kissing her partner and unbuttoning his shirt, biting his nipples and sliding her hands around him to scratch his back. "That's another thing that men are crazy for, having their backs scratched. If you scratch a man's back just this side of making it bleed, they love it. Ninety percent of them get a hard-on just from my doing that."

As I mentioned before, oral sex is a way of stimulating the eyes, as well as the penis, and Tessa is acutely aware that she is giving her lovers a performance. "I have very long hair, and if I went down on a guy's cock without pinning it back, he wouldn't be able to see a thing, only my hair bobbing up and down. I know how much men like to look, because every time I used to suck a guy's cock without pinning my hair back, he would keep on brushing it away from my face, over and over. When you give a guy oral sex, he wants to see his cock in your mouth. For him, that's the whole thrill of it.

"Once I've unbuttoned a guy's shirt, I push him back on the couch or the bed and I unbuckle his belt. He knows what's coming then, and I've never known a guy to resist, or try to take charge. He might run his hands through my hair or squeeze my breasts, but mostly he just lies back and lets it all happen. From my point of view, that's great, because it means that I have plenty of time to get aroused, and I've always been kind of slow when it comes to reaching orgasms. A man can play with my clitoris for almost forty-five minutes and I'm *nearly* there, do you know what I mean? Right on the very edge but not quite. Then suddenly it's like *whoomph*, and I have an orgasm, and after that I can go on having orgasms again and again.

"So for that reason, because I get aroused so slow, I don't like fucking at a hundred miles an hour, like most guys want to do it, so going down on a guy is perfect for that. I pull down his zipper and I open his pants, and I say, 'Who's hiding in here? There's definitely somebody hiding in here!' And I'll grab the guy's shorts and give his cock a good squeeze. You wouldn't believe it but men are like kids, they're watching me do this with their eyes all lit up like they're kids at a Christmas show.

"I'll say, 'I'm sure there's somebody in here, let's see who it is!' I mean the guy will be laughing but at the same time his cock will be sticking up like a broomstick. I'll say, 'Who is it, I wonder? Is it Little Peter?' But then I'll take it out of his shorts and I'll slide my hand all the way down it, all the way down to his balls, and say, 'No, it's not Little Peter . . . it's not Little Peter at all. It's Big Dick!'

"Did you say you wanted firsthand tips on sex? The first time you see a guy's cock, *always* say 'My God, you're enormous!' It doesn't matter if he's two inches shorter than the last guy you slept with, he's not to know, and unless you're stupid enough to tell him he's never going to find out. From my own personal experience, I would say that if a guy thinks *you* think that he's hung like a horse, it increases his libido by the power of ten.

"I know that men make comparisons with each other's cocks in locker rooms, and some guys get a complex because they think they're too small. But I think that you can totally negate all of that if you show him that you're impressed. I always go round-eyed when I first see a guy's cock—like, you know, 'You're going to *choke* me with this!' And I always give their cocks a nickname, so that I can pay their cock all of these compliments without it sounding too schmaltzy. For instance, you can't really say, 'Your penis is such a nice plum color, isn't it, Stephen?' without falling out of bed laughing. But you *can* say, 'Look at Big Dick! He's gone *purple!*'

"The first thing I do when I take a guy's cock out of his pants is stick my tongue right out and give it a big long lick, and look him straight in the face while I'm doing it. I try to give him a really wicked look, you know what I mean? Narrow my eyes, like 'This is so naughty, licking your cock, but ohhh . . . it's so tasty.'

"Then I hold his cock in my hand, right up under the bulgy bit, and I slide it across my lips, from side to side, with my mouth a little bit open, and my tongue sticking out. All the time I'm still staring at the guy, straight in the face. It's like I'm saying to him, 'Look at me, I've got your cock in my mouth, you're my king and I'm your slut.'

"You can feel it between your lips if a guy finds something really exciting because his cock can swell up very, very hard, even harder than normal, like it's just about to burst, and the hole will gape wide open like it's trying to breathe. And there's another way that you can tell, which is he'll push his hips up, like he's fucking you. Sometimes it's so subtle that you barely notice it, but it's like an involuntary kind of reaction, you know? A kind of a *twitch*.

"Another way of knowing when you've really hit the spot is by watching his eyes. Men love it when you lick the opening of their cock, around and around, with your tongue tip barely touching it. Their eyelids start to droop and they start breathing through their mouths and looking all hypnotized.

"It really turns them on when you slowly rub their cocks all over your face, too, all around your cheeks like you're putting on makeup. You can hold their cocks in front of your eyes and tickle them with your eyelashes. I knew a guy who loved climaxing over my eyelids. It really got him going when I had sperm dripping from my eyelashes. He used to suck it off and then he used to give me these long, slow kisses.

"After I've licked a guy's cock, I usually hold it in my hand and push it in and out of my mouth. It's kind of a cliché, I guess, but men get a real kick when they see their cocks making a bulge inside my cheek. I suck their cocks a little while I'm doing it, but not *too* hard, and I don't rub them too hard with my hand, either. I want this thing to *last*, right?

"Another thing I almost always do, which blows every man's mind, is I swallow their cocks as deep as I can. You only have to do it two or three times, and you don't have to take it all the way into your throat. I always make a gagging noise, and take their cocks out and say, 'Sorry . . . much too big.' I talked to a guy not long ago . . . I hadn't seen him for four years but the first thing he said was, 'I'll never forget that night you and me went out together. I almost choked you with my dick. I hope you've forgiven me.' I'll bet you he still goes around boasting to his friends that his cock is so enormous that he nearly choked me to death. But so what? Sex is all about fantasy, and making people feel excited."

Tessa plays games with the men in her life, but there is nothing mean or deceitful about the way she does it. Most of the men she dates want to get "down to business" straight away, but by giving them oral sex she defers intercourse and gets to know them and their sexual responses very much better. As a consequence, she is able to make their lovemaking last longer, and "ninety-seven percent of the time" she herself is fully satisfied. "Also . . . if I don't feel like having intercourse with the guy, or it's my period or something, I can suck him until he climaxes, and he's *still* happy."

Although Tessa has had sex with many men, she is now involved in what appears to have the makings of a long-term relationship with a young hotel manager, Frank. She uses similar techniques with Frank and their loving often lasts for hours. "Too many couples treat sex like a car crash. They come racing toward each other, then *smash!* and it's all over. Sex is finding out about somebody. Sex is giving another person pleasure way beyond anything they realized was possible. Sex is playacting, but it's playacting for your partner's entertainment. It should never be selfish. And you should always take your *time*."

There are dozens of ways in which you can use

your imagination not only to bring variety to your oral lovemaking, but also to exercise great control over your lover's staying power. One of the favorites is to crunch a few ice cubes between your teeth before you suck his cock, or to rinse your mouth with half-melted crushed ice. He will love the shock of chilly lips on warm penis, but at the same time it will numb his nerve endings and slow down his responses.

If you're not counting calories, you can use honey or molasses as a lubricant for oral sex, either by holding a spoonful in your mouth before you take him between your lips, or by smearing it all over his penis and enthusiastically licking it off. Lyle, 31, a teacher from St. Louis, Missouri, said that his wife Verna had poured maple syrup over his sexual organs one evening, when they were making love. "She massaged my balls with syrup and that was the stickiest, most erotic experience I ever had in my entire adult life. She even dipped her finger in syrup and stuck it up my ass."

Other additives to oral sex can include wine and liqueurs. "You can't say you're a connoisseur of anything until you've tasted a man's penis dipped in chilled champagne," said Olivia, 34, a sales assistant for a fashion store in San Diego, California. "It's romantic, as well as erotic." It turned out that Olivia's lover not only enjoyed a champagne dip, but he liked having his bare buttocks whipped with prickly rose stems at the same time. (For those whose budgets don't run to champagne, a good domestic sparkling wine will work just as well.)

You can give your man's penis a roughing up by coating your tongue with cookie-crumbs, too, or crushed nuts.

Although they may look very erotic, these oral performances are in fact designed to delay your partner's climax, rather than accelerate it. Men love to watch their penises being pampered, but licking is a comparatively mild form of stimulation, and most of the pleasure is visual.

Massage and another manipulations. Men play with their penises from the moment they're born. They don't do it for sexual stimulation alone, but also for reassurance, and almost as a form of meditation, like juggling with Zen balls. How many times have you seen a college professor, for example, with one hand in his pants pocket, absentmindedly fiddling with himself while he gives a lecture?

Obviously, there are no definitive surveys on the subject, but in thirty years of sexual counseling, I have yet to talk to a man who doesn't admit to playing with his penis in one way or another almost every single day, particularly when he's lying in bed at night thinking. Most of the time, even though he's fondling his penis, a man won't even have an erection. He's simply relaxing and enjoying the sensation in a similar way to a woman brushing out her hair.

Because they are external, men's penises are perceived as having a "personality" which women's vaginas, being far less visible, do not—even though vaginas are just as varied and characterful as penises. A well-known cartoon series, "Wicked Willie," featured a wisecracking penis, and throughout Asia disembodied phalluses with faces on them have been a feature of many different cultures for thousands of years. In the early 2000s two young entertainers toured theaters worldwide with a show called "Puppetry of the Penis," in which they stretched their sexual organs into various novelty shapes, such as the Eiffel Tower.

Your lover may not play with his penis in front of you, but you can be sure that he *does* play with it. It's also highly likely that he masturbates from time to time, especially if he's away on business quite a lot, or even if he simply wakes up in the night with a rigid penis and a head alive with sexual fantasies. He's not being unfaithful, even if he's not having fantasies about you. He's enjoying a quick, pleasurable release of sexual tension, just as millions of women do, when they're alone.

When you start regularly fondling your partner's penis, you're not just sexually stimulating him, you're joining a very personal meditation practice that he's been practicing all his life. Take hold of his penis in bed tonight and gently massage it (without the deliberate intention of making it erect, or making love). While you're doing this, ask him questions about his day at the office, or where he wants to take you on vacation, or who you ought to invite for a barbecue this weekend. Keep on fondling him as if it's the most natural thing in the world (and if you do it frequently enough, it eventually will be). You're directly plugging yourself in to one of the most basic circuits in his whole masculine character. You're showing an interest in him and discussing what he did all day, you're sympathizing with his problems, and at the same time you're soothing him and giving him pleasure by manipulating his penis.

He will quickly learn to associate your presence with calm, reassurance, and underlying sexual pleasure.

You can judge how strongly you ought to be massaging his penis by the way your conversation's going. It may become obvious that, although he's enjoying what you're doing, he's not in the mood for energetic sex. If he *does* show signs of interest, however, and you feel like it, too, you can stimulate him more and more strongly until he begins to stiffen. There are several different ways of doing this, and you will learn from trial and error which your lover responds to most quickly.

1) **The simple rhythmic rub.** Close your fist around his penis just around the ridge of his glans, and rub it rhythmically up and down, squeezing just a little harder on the upstroke. Don't make the mistake of doing this too quickly, or in flurried bursts, which many women do. Simply keep at it, with more or less the same pressure, and at more or less the same speed—one, *and*, two, *and*, three, *and*—

2) **The downstroke.** We've mentioned before that if you pull the skin of the penis firmly downward with each stroke you will stretch the frenum and the area directly below the corona, which can give a very pleasurable sensation. Hold your lover's penis in your fist and

rub it emphatically downward with each stroke, making sure that your knuckles beat very lightly on his testicles at the bottom of every stroke—not too hard, or you will make him jump about three feet in the air!

3) **The pincer.** Pinch the glans of his penis in between thumb and index finger, quite tightly, and rub up and down no more than an inch or two (25–50mm) in each direction. You should do this slightly more rapidly than the rhythmic rub. You will find that you can bring him to a climax quite quickly with the pincer, so be careful!

4) **The rolling pincer.** Again, pinch the glans of his penis in between thumb and index finger, but instead of rubbing it up and down, rotate the tip of your finger and the ball of your thumb counterclockwise, with a slow rolling motion. You can increase the strength of your pincer grip as your lover begins to show signs of approaching ejaculation (that's if you want him to ejaculate). You can also rotate your thumb and your finger harder so that you are twisting his glans from side to side, too. Both pincer movements can be done very lightly, so that a very pleasurable level of stimulation is maintained, but ejaculation is delayed for as long as you want it.

5) **The cage.** This is especially provocative if you have very long fingernails! Cup your hand over his glans and then lightly dig your fingernails into the skin of his penis just below

the corona. Move your hand up and down so that his glans rubs against the palm of your hand with every stroke. You can dig your nails in harder to see if he is stimulated by a little pain. There is a very fine line between hurting your lover so that he is sexually aroused and hurting him so much that you make his eyes water. As a general rule, you can dig your fingernails into his penis, and bite it, and you can scratch the skin of his scrotum, especially when he's very turned on. You can handle his testicles as long as you're reasonably gentle, but refrain from squeezing them hard or pulling on them violently. You can usually judge when you've reached the limit by his sharp intake of breath.

6) **Sexual knead.** Take the shaft of his penis in your fist and rhythmically squeeze it, as if you're kneading dough, pressing the ball of your thumb against the opening of his urethra. You can pull it a little, too, as if you're gently stretching it. When it's erect, you can also roll it between the palms of your hands, working your way upward until you're rolling his glans between your fingertips.

7) **Oils and creams.** Use scented massage oils or perfumed creams to rub his penis and his testicles. The best way of doing this is to have him lying naked on his back, while you kneel between his legs. You could add to the experience by lighting scented candles and playing exotic music. Again, this sounds as if it will

quickly bring him to a climax, but you can massage him very slowly and gently, so that while your performance *looks* highly erotic, the actual physical stimulation that you are giving him is really quite minimal. Imagine if your lover did the same thing to you, stroking the lips of your vulva, but barely touching your clitoris at all. You'd enjoy it, but it wouldn't immediately bring you to an orgasm. Talking of oils and creams, a man who suffers from premature ejaculation may be prescribed an anesthetic cream by his doctor to rub on his penis before intercourse. This cream usually contains lignocaine, and it has the effect of numbing his penis. An even older method of delaying a man's climax is to apply a spot of Tiger Balm to his scrotum and the tip of his penis. Tiger Balm is an ancient Chinese cure for almost everything, from rheumatism to hay fever, with a strong aromatic smell. You can buy it in Chinese pharmacies, or else if you're an amateur chemist you can make your own out of menthol crystals, camphor blocks, beeswax, petroleum jelly, oil of cloves, oil of cajuput, oil of cinnamon and ammonium hydroxide. The effect on the penis is a cold, burning sensation, and a very long-lasting erection.

8) **The love glove.** Many men are very aroused by having their penises massaged by a woman wearing gloves. You can experiment with all kinds of different gloves—latex, leather, vinyl, lace—even knobbly golfing gloves.

9) **Toys for boys.** Internet sex-aid catalogs advertise all kinds of toys which you can use to stimulate your partner's penis. You can buy simple electric vibrators which you attach to the backs of your fingers, to make them buzz when you touch him; or else you can choose from a bewildering selection of plastic penises, including ones that pump up and down, ones that light up, and ones that ejaculate whatever liquid you care to fill them up with. There are also artificial vaginas, some of them fairly plain and straightforward, others allegedly modeled on the real vaginas of famous porn stars. On the whole, the most practical choice is probably the penis-shaped vibrator, since you can use this to give him a buzzing massage around his penis and his testicles. If it's well lubricated with KY, you can also push it into his anus while you're masturbating him or giving him oral sex, or when you're actually having intercourse—so that you're entering *him* while he's entering *you*. You can use it yourself, too, to give him a highly graphic display of vaginal or anal penetration. You know how aroused men are by *looking*. However, there are even more dramatic uses for the penis-shaped vibrator, which we shall talk about later.

10) **Underwater.** Manipulating your partner's penis in a swimming pool or in the ocean can give him a very special *frisson*. It's a very good way to play with him and get him erect without there being any pressure on either of you to go

all the way, since pools and beaches are often within sight of other people, and in any case intercourse underwater can be extremely difficult because of the lack of sexual lubricants. Libby, 24, a singer from San Bernardino, California, said, "I love playing with my boyfriend's cock in the swimming pool. It's the best tease ever. You can get him so hard, so that he's absolutely panting for it, but all you have to do is swim away!"

Try to become so familiar with your partner's penis that you almost imagine it's part of you, and so that he grows totally relaxed about your frequent fondling. In this way, you'll be able to take control of your lovemaking as if it's the most natural thing in the world. By "taking control," I mean that if you want to, *you* can choose when to make love, and where, and how, and how long it lasts. Maybe you won't want to make those choices every time you have sex. You probably won't need to. But at least you'll have the ability to do it.

The frequent fondling program really comes into its own when a man has trouble getting erections, or suffers from any other sexual difficulties. If you manipulate his penis fairly regularly, you're less likely to find that he suddenly and inexplicably turns his back on you in bed, as so many women do. How many times has a woman said to me, "I couldn't understand what was wrong . . . I thought there was something wrong with *me*"? But you'll be closely in touch with his sexual ups and downs, and whatever problems he suffers, you'll be much better equipped to help him get over them. It's almost impossible for your partner to keep secrets about erectile dysfunction if you play with his penis more often than he does.

Your importance in the care and maintenance of your partner's penis can never be exaggerated. When couples' relationships break up because the man is unable to perform in bed, it is almost always because he refused to discuss with his partner what was wrong. But if you have taken the trouble to develop an intimate, ongoing relationship with Mr. Sausage right from the very start of your relationship, you will be aware at once when he isn't rising to the occasion.

Patricia, a 33-year-old hairdresser from Phoenix, Arizona, was a classic example. Her husband John, a 36-year-old electrical engineer, was involved in a serious auto accident eighteen months after they were married and began to have difficulty in getting erections. ED isn't at all uncommon after any traumatic experience, such as bereavement, or divorce—or in John's case, a very close brush with death.

"John is very good-looking, and he's always been husky and fit. He works out, he plays tennis. Certainly not the kind of guy that a woman would look at and think, he can't get it up.

"We had a great sex life when we first got married. John would come home from work and he would pick me up in his arms and carry me off to the couch. He used to tear my clothes off, literally, to the point where I stopped wearing any panties when I was expecting him back. He would fuck me everywhere: in the living room, in the kitchen, halfway up the stairs, bending down in the shower. I couldn't even take the bed linen down to the laundry room without him following me and fucking me on the floor on a big heap of crumpled sheets.

"I didn't have too many boyfriends before John, so it isn't all that easy for me to make comparisons, but I would say that his cock is someplace between 'good-sized' and 'big.' When he's really turned on, it seems to get bigger than ever. It certainly fills me right up, let's say that.

"He was fine for about a month after the accident, but he'd broken his ankle so he couldn't come home like he used to and pick me up. Then one night in bed he put his arm around me and started to kiss me but he couldn't seem to get a boner. I tried rubbing it for him but it still didn't get hard. He said it was probably the painkillers he was taking, and he'd be better in the morning. But the next morning he got out of bed before I woke up, and when he came home in the evening he didn't try to make love to me, either.

"I think he made one more attempt, on Sunday morning, real early, maybe five o'clock. He had a boner then, and he climbed on top of me and put it inside me, and it was great, it was really big, and when he started to fuck me he picked me right off the bed so that his cock went right up inside me as far as it could go.

"Suddenly, though, I could feel it dying away, and the next thing I knew it had slipped right out of me.

John kept saying sorry, sorry, and trying to rub his cock with his hand, but it wouldn't get hard. I told him not to worry, it was probably the pills, and as soon as he stopped taking them, everything would be okay. But he said he *had* stopped taking them, about four days before. He turned his back to me and I was left lying there wondering what was wrong.

"Let me tell you, things went from bad to worse. I didn't think that John had fallen out of love with me, or anything like that, but I did think that he had a pretty serious problem. Not being able to get an erection, you've no idea how much that changed him. It made him a *smaller man*, if you understand what I mean. It was like he walked around everywhere with his head bent and his shoulders hunched, and any time one of his friends told a blue joke, he laughed, but he always looked kind of desperate— like, 'All of these guys are laughing at sex, and I can't even get a boner.'

"That's why I'm so pleased that I talked to you. I took your advice and even when he turned his back on me, I cuddled up close to him, and slid my hand into his pajamas and fondled his cock. And, like you said, I did it real gentle, almost absentminded, and I kept the conversation real low-key, like 'How were things at work today . . . did you get that contract completed?'

"At first I could tell that he didn't want me to touch him, but I kept at it, and one morning when he was in the shower I took off my clothes and joined him, and I soaped him all over and kissed him and soaped his cock and his balls. He began to get this enormous boner but I didn't rush him, and after a while I said that I had to get to work, so I stepped out of the shower and dried myself and got dressed.

"I think he was ready then to make love to me. When he stepped out of the shower after me, his cock was still sticking right up. I gave it a squeeze and kissed him again and said, 'See you tonight,' and left the situation like that, which was good, because it meant that he wasn't pressured into thinking he had to make love to me, right then and there, just because I'd joined him in the shower.

"It worked better than I expected. When he came home that night, I went into the bedroom while he was changing. He was wearing nothing but his shirt and his shorts. I kissed him and slid my hand into his shorts, and started to rub his cock up and down the way you told me, very slow. I only had to rub him two or three times before he got a boner. I knelt down on the carpet in front of him and pulled down his shorts and started to suck his cock. It was so long since I'd done it, it was heaven. I licked him all over, and nuzzled his balls. And again, I didn't rush it, or make out like I was in a hurry for him to come.

"After a while he picked me up and laid me down on the bed. He lifted my skirt and he pulled my panties to one side, and he was about to climb on top of me but I remembered what you'd said about the first time you have intercourse after you've had some problems. I said, 'No . . . I'm getting on top,' and I rolled him over so that he was lying on his back.

"I took his cock in my hand and steered it into my

pussy. Ohhh, that felt good, and I let him know it. I sat up straight so that his cock went right up inside me as far as it could go. But I did like you told me and I didn't ride him up and down. I just sat there and enjoyed the feeling of being filled up with cock.

"He kept trying to lift up his hips, to fuck me, and I let him do it, but I didn't join in . . . well, not the way I used to, like a bucking bronco! I leaned forward and held him close, and just let him slide his cock gently in and out of me. After a while, his boner started to get soft, and it slipped out of me, but I kept on holding him close, and I said, 'That was perfect.' Which it had been, you know? if you don't think that you *have* to have a climax every time you make love."

The technique which I suggested to Patricia is part of a program technically known as "sensate focus." It is intended to remove any pressure on the man to maintain an erection or to reach a climax. Once he can achieve an erection and keep it inside his partner's vagina without losing it, he can then progress to stimulation and ejaculation.

During the rise of feminism in the 1960s and 1970s, so much emphasis was placed on the right of women to have orgasms like men that "satisfaction" and "fulfillment" came to be accepted as essential goals. While orgasms and climaxes are obviously enjoyable and desirable, the physical and emotional communication of sex is much more important . . . the unconditional giving of one personality to another, the sharing of desires and fantasies and dreams.

Really close sexual communication comes through

"The World's Sexiest Men" have clearly indicated that a couple of extra inches in the pants department are, on the whole, irrelevant.

Charm, self-confidence and good looks all score highly—although I have to emphasize that "good looks" doesn't necessarily mean classical good looks. Gemma, a 25-year-old photographic model from New York, said, "The size of a man's cock doesn't come into it. I've been with big men and average men and slightly-less-than-average men, but I can put my hand on my heart and swear to you that I didn't notice any difference at all when it came to having sex. Oh, except for one guy, Jamie, who was actually *shorter* than me, but his cock was very thick, and sometimes I used to find it really uncomfortable when he first pushed himself inside me. He tried to have anal sex with me once, but I said, no way. I wouldn't have been able to sit down for a week." As for looks? "I don't like pretty men. I go for men who look as if they've been around a bit—you know, battered. I like blue eyes and scruffy hair and hoarse voices. I just love men with hoarse voices."

So as far as Gemma's concerned, it looks as if a man would have more chance of getting her into bed if he smoked sixty Camels a day, rather than spending his money on ways to enlarge his penis.

Obviously, many women find the sight of a very large erect penis to be exciting, but women's sexual responses are not as visual as men's. Men can be aroused by a photograph of a vulva even though they can't see the face of the woman it belongs to, whereas women tend to be much more sexually attracted by a man's general appearance and sexual charisma.

It is also noteworthy that when it comes to intercourse, the women to whom I have spoken over the years show a distinct preference for *thick* penises rather than *long* penises . . . so men with short stubby ones don't have anything to worry about.

If you have never expressed any disappointment in the size of your partner's penis, then why is *he* so concerned about its size? The answer is that he has probably had a humiliating experience at some time or other in a locker room—when he was very much younger, maybe, and his penis wasn't as developed as some of his classmates'. Or maybe he has seen other men naked at the golf club and considered that his penis was smaller than theirs.

One very common reason why men think that their penises are too small is because they are overweight, and the root of their (perfectly normal) penis is buried in a pillowy bulge of abdominal fat. If they could manage to lose a few pounds off their waistline, they would discover that they look just as well equipped as other men.

A man's height and physical stature gives you absolutely no clue to the size of his penis. A huge man can have a very small penis—and by comparison with the rest of his body, it will look even smaller. On the other hand, a small man can have a very large penis. Frank Sinatra was said by his valet to have a penis so large that whenever he wore evening dress he put on a woman's panty girdle to keep himself strapped in. When I was undertaking sex research in Sweden in the 1970s, I came across a dwarf in a German circus who had the largest penis that I have ever seen before or since. He used to joke that his sex life was terrible because every time he had an erection he used to faint from loss of blood.

Despite the old wives' tales, there is also no link whatsoever between the size of a man's penis or the size of his nose (or his feet).

In actual fact, men's penises don't vary in size all that much, and many modern sexologists prefer to measure them in volume, or filling capacity, rather than length and circumference. This generally ranges from 5.7 to 28.8 cubic inches (94–423cc).

As you have probably seen for yourself, your partner's penis can vary considerably in size even when it's soft. On a chilly day, even the penis of a fully grown man can shrink to no bigger than a cherub's in a Renaissance painting, especially since his scrotum will have tightened up and retracted his testicles close to the warmth of his body. But if the surroundings are warm and your partner is feeling relaxed, his penis can be quite plump and swollen, and his testicles will be hanging down lower to give an added impression of size.

Unless a man's penis is so small that he is unable to have intercourse, which is extremely rare indeed, then there is no need for him (or you) to worry about the size of his penis. As somebody once remarked, "What do you mean, your penis is too short? It reaches your body, doesn't it?"

Having said that, however, men *do* worry about

the size of their penises, whether their anxiety is justified or not. They worry so much, in fact, that penis-enlargement products and exercise programs have become a multimillion-dollar worldwide industry. (It's all interconnected with the impotence industry, too, since men who are concerned about their penis size often suffer from erection problems as a consequence.)

The size of a man's penis doesn't strictly matter any more than the size of a woman's breasts strictly matter. But they're both a question of self-image, and self-image is a vital part of masculinity and femininity, and of a person's sexuality as a whole. No matter how illogical it may be for a man to fret about what he perceives as his smaller-than-average penis, it can seriously affect his sexual confidence, and have a disproportionately damaging effect on his relationships.

It won't be easy for you to find out if your partner has an inferiority complex about the size of his penis. If you thought that it was difficult to coax a man to talk about his erection problems, just try asking him if his penis is too small. But there *are* ways of telling if it's preying on his mind.

First, when you look at him naked, do you think that compared to other men his penis appears very small/small/average/large/enormous? No matter how much you love him and fancy him, try to be objective.

Second, does he openly undress in front of you so that you can clearly see his penis, or does he always get undressed hurriedly, or in the dark, or in another room?

Third, does he usually make love to you with the lights off, or under the bedcovers?

Fourth, does he avoid putting himself in a position in which you might be tempted to give him oral sex?

Fifth, does he obviously enjoy it when you fondle his penis, or do you feel that he tries to discourage you from doing it?

Sixth, does he dislike watching pornographic videos with naked men in them?

Seventh, is he unreasonably jealous if you talk to other men at parties, etc.?

Eighth, how often does he lose his erection in the middle of intercourse: often/occasionally/never?

Ninth, is he unusually aggressive in the way that he makes love?

Tenth, is he generally aggressive in his day-to-day behavior for no apparent reason?

Eleventh, is he obsessive about working out and physical development?

Twelfth, is he extra fastidious about his grooming and appearance?

Thirteenth, after making love, does he always ensure that he gets dressed again, or puts on pajamas or shorts?

Of course, none of these is a 100 percent guarantee that your partner is worried about the size of his penis. But your answer to the first question will tell you if he has real or perceived reason to feel that he is smaller than average, and the remaining questions will tell you something about his sexual self-confidence, or his lack of it. Men who appear to have a chip on their shoulder, or who behave rudely or aggressively to women for no discernible reason, are often concerned about their sexuality. They might in reality be very shy, and their obnoxiousness is a way of covering it up. They might be confused about their sexual orientation. But judging by the global sales figures of penis-enlargement pills and penis-stretching gadgets, literally hundreds of thousands of men feel that their penises are too small. They are so desperate to increase the size of their penises that they are prepared to part with hundreds of dollars, with no guarantee that they're going to end up anything other than sore, or blistered, or even worse, and not a millionth of an inch longer.

So—if you suspect that your partner may be worried about the size of his penis, what can you do?

Here's Shanii, 27, a Realtor from La Jolla, California: "I always liked Dave from the day I first met him at a realty convention in San Diego. He has these dark good looks that I really go for, so that he always looks like he needs a shave. I thought he was so attractive and I couldn't understand why he was so quiet and shy. You know, I looked at him, and I thought 'This guy could take his pick of any girl he wanted.'

"We got talking during the coffee break, and I could tell that he liked me. We traded phone numbers and e-mail addresses but he didn't ask to see me again and days went by and he didn't call me. In the end I e-mailed him at his office and told him that I had two tickets for a concert and would he like to come along? I had never done that before, I mean, *me,* asking a guy out?

"But—we had a really great date. The concert was fabulous, and afterward we had a meal overlooking the bay. Dave drove me back to my apartment and I invited him in. I really liked him, you know, and I was giving him all the signals. We had a couple of glasses of wine, and I put on a Moby CD. He kissed me and unbuttoned my dress and I thought, now I'm getting someplace. He's strong but he's very tender, and a very good kisser.

"He unfastened my bra and kissed my breasts and sucked at my nipples. I'm a sucker for having my nipples sucked! I opened his shirt and ran my fingers through the hair on his chest. He's so sexy, his chest is shaggy like a beast out of the forest. He took off my thong and he slid his hand in between my legs and ran the tip of his finger up my slit, and that really made me shiver.

"I started to unbuckle his belt. I could tell from the way his pants were straining that he was hard. But he said, 'No, let's do it with the lights down low . . . more romantic.' By that time romance was just about the last thing on my mind, but I didn't argue. He turned off all the lights except for the lava lamp on the coffee table, and then he quickly took off his socks and his pants. He sat on the couch next to me and held up a condom packet and said, 'Safety first.' I said, 'Give it to me, let me put it on for you,' because you know how much men like it when you roll their condom on for them, but he said, 'No, you're okay,' and before I knew it he had done it himself.

"I ran my hands through his hair and I massaged

his shoulders and all the way down his back. He has a great body. He's not muscly but he doesn't have a single spare ounce of fat. I dug my fingernails in the cheeks of his ass, and I could tell he liked it, but when I started to reach around to touch his cock, he grabbed hold of my wrists and lifted my arms way up over my head. He kind of pinned me down on the couch like that. He wasn't hurting me or anything, but I couldn't reach down to touch him.

"He kissed me, and got on top of me. He had to let go of one of my wrists for a moment so that he could position his cock into my cunt. I tried to put my hand down to help him, but he grabbed me again so that I couldn't. He pushed himself inside me and I'll tell you, it felt *fabulous*. He's a good lover, he really takes it easy, so that his cock goes in and out like he's swimming or something, in and out, gradually working you up to it. The only thing I didn't like was the way he kept my wrists pinned up over my head. I usually like to play with a guy's balls when he's making love to me, and sometimes I like to stretch my cunt lips wide open with my fingers, and stroke my clitoris to help me come.

"I didn't come that time, and he didn't even notice. When he was finished he climbed off me right away. You expect to lie there in each other's arms for a few minutes, don't you, sweating and panting and kissing and telling each other how great it was? But Dave had taken off his condom and put his shorts and his pants back on before I had time to ask him if he wanted a shower.

"He poured us another glass of wine and he sat

next to me and stroked my hair and kissed me and told me how beautiful I was. *I* didn't get dressed . . . I love lying there naked after making love. I couldn't understand why he had wanted to get dressed so quick. I asked him if he would like to stay the night but he told me he had an eight-thirty meeting in LA."

Shanii was baffled by Dave's behavior. It was clear that he found her very attractive, and he asked to meet her again the following evening. He took her into downtown San Diego, where they had dinner and drinks, and he drove her home. Neither of them could wait to get into bed and make love, but Dave still contrived to make sure that the lights were very low, and to roll on his own condom, and to hold her in such a way that she found it almost impossible to touch his penis.

"I couldn't understand it. I felt like he was trying to hide something from me. I began to wonder if there was something wrong with his cock, like some kind of disfigurement. So the next time we went to bed, and he tried to take hold of my wrists, I said, 'No! Let me go,' and I sat up and switched on the lights. He was kneeling on the bed with his hands between his legs and he was looking at me like I'd caught him doing something really embarrassing, you know?

"I said, 'What's going on? Why do we have to make love in the dark? Why won't you let me touch your cock?'

"I couldn't believe it when he told me. He said, 'I didn't want you to see it because it's not very big.'

I said, '*What?*' I mean, it *felt* big enough, when it was inside me. I took his hands away, one after the other, and there was all this shaggy black hair, and sticking out of this shaggy black hair was a perfectly ordinary cock. It wasn't 9 inches long or anything. Maybe you could have called it a little stubby. But it was 5 inches long, at least, and it was good and thick, and what more could you want?

"I took hold of it, and rubbed it, and it was lovely and hard, and I just looked at him and said, 'You're crazy. This is a great cock.' He tried to get up but I pushed him onto his back and I went on rubbing him up and down. I said, 'Come on, you have to tell me the whole story about this, or I'll stop.' "

Dave eventually told Shanii that he had reached puberty comparatively late, and that he had been teased at school about his undeveloped penis and his lack of pubic hair. Even when he had matured, he had remained intensely self-conscious about his sexual organs, and had always believed that his penis was smaller than that of other men.

In fact, Dave was suffering from the problem that afflicts 99.9 percent of men who are convinced that they have an undersized penis—a lack of sexual self-confidence. It can take only one incident of teasing or one slighting remark to affect a man for the rest of his life. Bill, a 29-year-old payroll clerk from Detroit, Michigan, told me that when he was dumped by his girlfriend for another man, her parting remark was, "Anyhow . . . Oliver's cock is twice the size of yours!"

"It was bad enough that I had lost her," said Bill.

"I really loved that girl, and I always thought that we were going to get married. When she said that I had a small cock, of course I believed her, and I thought that was why she had left me. I developed a terrible complex about the size of my cock, and I didn't date girls for nearly two years after that. I got so depressed about it that I was on pills, and of course that didn't help my sex life, either, because I had trouble in getting erections. I was seriously considering surgery to have my penis enlarged."

Of course Bill's penis was a perfectly good size, but like most men he was intensely self-conscious about it. It took a consultation with a specialist to reassure him that he needed no enlargement treatment, and that he was capable of satisfying any woman who wanted to go to bed with him. Even after this he was still not totally sure of himself, so he visited three different prostitutes. "Not one of them made any comment about the size of my cock, and one of them actually said, 'My God, you're a big boy, aren't you?'"

Sounds ridiculous? It may, but we all have anxieties of one kind or another, and we all need reassurance, from time to time. That's what I told Shanii, and as a result she treated Dave to an ongoing program of frequent fondling, so that he was in no doubt at all that she found his penis more than adequate. I recommended that she play with his penis while he was lying on his back, and pull it directly upward in regular, rhythmic tugs, so that he could see for himself how far she was stretching it. I also recommended that she lick and suck his penis, making a particular show of licking all the way down the underside from his glans to his testicles, to give an added impression of length. She also (successfully) tried Tessa's trick of taking his whole penis into her mouth, but pretending to choke because of its size. "Sorry . . . you're just too big for me."

Apart from glimpses in the golf club locker room, or pornographic videos, men get very few opportunities to compare penis sizes with other men, and these are never conducted under scientifically controlled conditions. In other words, they are never at the same ambient temperature, or at the same stage of sexual arousal, or with their bladders equally full.

Because of that, your partner relies on you much more than you think to give him an objective opinion of how large his penis is. So even if you consider that it's only about average, what are you going to tell him? Of course you are. With just a few admiring words, you can make your man feel like a prize stallion. You may think that it's slightly dishonest, but just think how much *you* enjoy receiving compliments. And, believe me, *you'll* reap the benefit of it.

What do you do if your lover still seems to be dissatisfied with the size of his penis . . . or if he simply hankers to have an extra-big one? Well, human beings are never rational, especially when it comes to sexual self-image. As the editor of several men's magazines, I met countless very pretty girls who had undergone breast enlargement, some of them several times, so that their breasts were stratospheric. Nobody had bullied or cajoled them into doing it. Enormous breasts weren't even a prerequisite for being a centerfold. They had done it because it made them feel special, and more attractive. They loved knowing that every man's eyes were on them when they walked down the street in a tight T-shirt. And all I can say is, if it made them happy, and it caused them no physical problems, where was the harm?

Similarly, there is no harm at all in a man trying to make his penis bigger (except by surgery, which we will deal with later.) There are hundreds of different methods of penis enlargement on offer—exercise programs, herbal pills, creams, lotions, sprays, vacuum pumps, stretchers and mechanical rollers.

It can cost anything from $20 to $100 to join a penis-enlargement site on the Internet. Most of these offer herbal medication or a course of exercises, some of them "derived from the rituals of ancient African tribes that were passed down from father to son,"—others based on "space-age aerobics designed to increase astronauts' lung capacity." All of them promise a "humongous snake" or a "hefty peter."

"You'll radiate confidence and success whenever you enter a locker room, and other men will look at you with real envy. But the best part is when you reveal yourself in all your glory to the woman in your life. When she sees how massive and manly, how truly long and hard you are, she will surrender and give you everything you always wanted. As you drive your penis deep inside her she'll gasp as you dominate her. If you have a penis that is 7, 8 or even

9 inches long, you will be able to penetrate the more sensitive areas of a woman and reach nerve endings that she probably doesn't even know she has!"

It's good advertising copy, isn't it? It deals right at the start with the *real* reason why most men want a larger penis—so that they're not embarrassed to show their dinkles off in those infamous locker rooms, in front of other men. Just imagine standing in the showers next to the CEO, and your penis is twice as big as his! Then it gives the impression that a larger penis somehow makes women swoon in submission, and "awesomely" improves a man's sex technique, "enabling him to reach her most sensitive area of all—the famous G-spot."

Some penis-enlargement sites offer extras such as instructional videos and "men's health" tips, as well as advice on lovemaking. Almost all of them display testimonials from delighted guys who have added 1½–2 inches to their penises in less than a year. One site at least has the honesty to say that "if you think you can grow an additional 4 inches in length, we've got some land in Florida we'd like to sell you." But another cautions that "a penis larger than 9 inches may be too large for most women . . . but if for some reason you need even more, it is possible for you to safely continue taking our product."

If your lover wants to try any of the commercial methods which claim to enlarge men's penises, I think he should choose the most pleasurable. That way, at least he'll get some fun for his money. Frequent manipulation is good for a man's penis, especially in middle age and later life, and so "enlargement exercises" will certainly be beneficial, even if they don't make his penis any bigger.

During the course of preparing this book, I have personally tried a wide selection of penis-enlargement medications, as well as some of the most popular penis-enlarging devices and a whole range of penis-enlarging exercises from "ancient" to "space-age."

I have followed all of the instructions to the letter, and been patient and persistent. All I can say at the conclusion of my tests is that either my penis is already so large that it simply can't be increased in size any further, or else I suffer from some physiological abnormality which renders my penis completely impervious to pills, pumps or any other method of making it bigger.

In nearly two years of tests, I can report no permanent increase in penis size whatsoever, either length or girth. Of course I am not suggesting that the methods I tried are not effective for other men. But if your lover is determined to embark on a course of penis enlargement, I would advise him from my own experience not to expect too much from it. Older readers may remember the "X-Ray Spex" that used to be advertised in comic books, which would enable men to see through women's clothing. I suspect that some of the penis-enlargement products on the market are made by the same people.

You know that your lover doesn't really need a bigger penis, but if it makes him happy to have a try, these are some of the methods on the market:

Penis-enlargement pills: You can buy any number of patented "doctor-approved" pills which claim to give you "a MUCH larger penis in thickness and length," not forgetting a "rock-solid erection."

These are marketed under names like VigRx, Extagen, Magna RX, Longitude, Enzyte, SizeMAX and Androenlarge. Although none of them worked for me, some penis-enlargement enthusiasts on the Internet say that they have noticed gains in size, "although it takes a few months before these become noticeable."

Most of these pills come with a 100 percent moneyback guarantee, so theoretically your lover has nothing to lose if his penis doesn't grow any bigger, or if he doesn't get "rock-hard" erections.

I talked to a group of top urologists who have formed the world's first men's-health forum in Bristol, England, with the specific aim of improving men's sex lives. One of its members, Tim Whittlestone, said, "There are many herbal remedies and supplements advertised, but no widely accepted evidence that they work." However, he wouldn't rule out a placebo effect. In other words, if your lover *thinks* that an herbal pill can improve his potency, then it may very well do so. As we have seen, a man's sexual performance is very much affected by his state of mind.

Mr. Whittlestone also refused to discount the benefits of gingko biloba, which improves blood circulation, and ginseng root, which is a stimulant. These may help your lover to achieve an erection, and his penis may appear to be larger than normal because of improved blood flow, but there is no research to indicate that this increase will be permanent.

A typical penis-enlargement pill will contain all or some of the following ingredients:

Ginkgo biloba: also known as the maidenhair tree. The seeds and leaves of ginkgo biloba relax and dilate blood vessels, and so improve the circulation.

Korean red ginseng: ginseng is a form of ivy, and its root contains vitamins B_1, B_2, biotin, B_3, B_5, A, E, rutin and the minerals calcium, iron, phosphorus, sodium, silicon, potassium, manganese, magnesium, sulfur, tin and germanium. It is said to increase the flow of blood to the brain and the penis, and to stimulate the formation of red blood cells.

Cuscuta seed: is thought to strengthen bones, nourish sperm and increase fertility, as well as improve the eyesight.

Saw palmetto: also known as sabal, the saw palmetto contains vitamin A, along with alkaloids, resins, dextrin, glucose and active oils. It is traditionally used to stimulate male sex hormones.

Epimedium sagittum: also known as "Yang tonic" or "horny goat weed," this herb is supposed to give warm, pleasurable feelings and act as an aphrodisiac.

Hawthorn berry: hawthorn berries are supposed to have the effect of normalizing your circulatory system—either stimulating it or depressing it, according to what it needs.

Catuaba: an herbal tonic from Brazil which is said to fortify the nervous system and relieve fatigue. Regular use is also supposed to give erotic dreams.

Muira pauma: a tree which also grows in Brazil and is often used in conjunction with catuaba to tone up the male genitourinary system and to ward off impotence.

Orchic substance: an extract from bulls' testicles, which is said to increase testosterone levels.

Oyster meat extract: oysters contain phosphorus, iodine and zinc, and are traditionally thought to be an aphrodisiac.

The cost of taking penis-enlargement pills is approximately sixty dollars a month. Your lover might consider that there are other things he would rather buy for sixty dollars a month, but the choice is his.

Penis pump: this is a transparent acrylic cylinder fitted with an airtight seal, into which your lover inserts his penis. He then extracts air from the cylinder with a manual or an electric vacuum pump. Blood is drawn into his penis to fill the vacuum, and lo and behold, he has a huge erection!

Penis pumps can be very useful for men who have difficulty in achieving an erection and can't take medication. The usual procedure is for the man to give himself a hard-on with his penis pump, and then attach a constricting rubber ring around the base of his penis to prevent the blood inside it from flowing back into his body.

Although penis pumps take much of the spontaneity out of lovemaking, and some women complain that they make a man's penis feel uncomfortably cold, they can be a very effective way of achieving a quick stiffie.

However, penis pumps are also commonly used for penis enlargement. The idea is that your lover should "pump" himself three or four times a week over a period of several months, gradually increasing the vacuum pressure and the length of time that his penis remains inside the cylinder. Dedicated penis pumpers are convinced that the tissue inside their penises will adapt over time to accommodate much more blood, making their penises permanently thicker. They also believe that the suspensory ligaments which attach the penis to the pubic bone will be stretched—giving a lasting increase in length, too.

I talked to several hardened pumpers who claimed to have gained ¾ to 1 inch in length and (in one case) over 2 inches in circumference. But it became clear that this had taken them years of concentrated effort, and that the "miracles" of penis enlargement promised by some penis-pump purveyors were highly exaggerated.

"I'll be frank with you," said Joe, a 37-year-old sound recording technician from Sherman Oaks, California. "I do it because I enjoy it. It gives me a good feeling about myself, because when it's all pumped up my cock grows huge, and I think the exercise is good for my circulation."

Joe acknowledged that three and a half years of pumping had not added even a fraction of an inch to the size of his penis, but it did remain much larger than normal for two or three hours after a pumping session. "I always pump before I go out on a date, which makes me feel very confident, because my pants are bulging, and I try to do it before I take a woman to bed, although it isn't always easy to find an excuse to go into another room to pump myself up."

When he did manage to pump his penis immediately before having intercourse, he found that his penis was larger and firmer, and that his erections lasted longer than normal.

Richard, 44, an accountant from Cleveland, Ohio, said that he had bought a penis pump without his wife's knowledge. He felt that their sex life had become routine and unexciting, and he imagined that a larger penis would impress her. "I pumped my cock up just before we went to bed. She was sitting up in bed reading her book. I got into bed beside her, took her book away from her, and lifted her glasses off her nose. She said, 'Hey, what's up?' and I said, '*This* is up.' I took hold of her hand and put it on my cock. When she felt it, her eyes went wide. She pulled down the covers and took a look at it and said, '*Wow.*' I'll tell you, we had a really great time that night. We made love in all kinds of positions . . . doggy-style, everything. She kept telling me how horny I was, and I *did* feel horny, because my cock was so big and it seemed to stay hard for hours."

After using the pump three or four times, Richard told his wife what he was doing, and why. Far from being upset, she was very enthusiastic, and encouraged him to go on using it whenever they made love.

"She likes to watch me pumping my cock, and when it gets to full size she can't wait to get her hands on it. Sometimes she comes into my study when I'm working at the weekends and says, 'Come on, let's do it now.' I don't think I've actually gained any inches, but my sex life has sure taken a turn for the better. When you live with somebody for years,

I guess it's easy to get into a rut, and sometimes you need something to shake you out of it."

If your lover is attracted to the idea of a penis pump, however, he should be careful not to overdo it. Some men are in too much of a hurry to get that humongous snake, and because of that they tend to pump their penises too frequently, and keep them swollen for too long, with far too much vacuum pressure applied. By doing this they expose themselves to the risk of rupturing their capillaries and other blood vessels. If large bruises appear on the shaft of your lover's penis, or scarlet spots develop on his glans, then he should stop pumping until they disappear . . . and this can take quite a few days.

Your lover may also find that the skin on his penis turns darker, or watery blisters appear on the surface. Also, he may find that his erections become less frequent and much flabbier, and that they last only a few minutes before they subside. In extreme cases, there is a danger of severe internal bleeding.

If he's *still* determined to try pumping, he should make sure that he buys a high-quality pump with an accurate pressure gauge. A good manual pump can cost two hundred dollars and an electric pump almost six hundred dollars. The cylinder should be 2–3 inches longer than the normal length of his erect penis, and not more than 1 inch wider in circumference, to ensure a good seal. If your lover is exceptionally large or exceptionally small, some manufacturers will produce a cylinder to order.

Penis-enlargement P.E.: Many advertisers offer penis-enlargement exercises, and almost all of these are "secret techniques from the Orient." Most of them are also remarkably similar. There are only so many ways in which your lover can masturbate, after all.

Some exercises are quite elaborate, and involve rolling the penis against the floor or slapping it from side to side. The basic exercise, however, is what you might call "milking." The penis should be firmly gripped at the base and then rhythmically squeezed-and-pulled all the way toward the glans. This action should be repeated twenty or thirty times, or until your lover climaxes, or until he grows bored.

There are very good reasons why a man should keep his penis well exercised (or any other part of his body, for that matter). Even the most skeptical of sex advisors warn older men to "use it or lose it." But if a man has to go without sexual intercourse for any length of time, regular masturbation is quite sufficient, using whichever grip he happens to prefer.

The idea behind "milking" is to stimulate the flow of blood into the penis, to make it thicker, and to stretch the ligaments, so that it becomes longer.

There is even a special device on the market called a "Power-Jelq" which your lover can use to "milk" or "jelq" his penis. The Power-Jelq is a pair of soft foam rollers attached to hinged metal handles. Your lover places his penis in between the rollers and then the handles are squeezed together so that the rollers lock. He then rhythmically pulls the rollers down the length of his penis, releases the lock, and repeats the action as many times as he desires.

"The soft foam-covered rollers will form to the

shape of the penile shaft and create a seal, similar to wrapping the index finger and thumb around the penis using the 'OK' grip. The foam is made of sturdy closed-cell polyethylene, and will not soak up water or lubrication. The Power-Jelq device is safe to use in the shower!"

Although it does get somewhat monotonous after a while, the sensation of using the Power-Jelq is not entirely unpleasant, and you might like to buy one for your lover as an amusement. It costs only $39.95, after all, and even if his penis shows no signs of enlargement, you might have some fun with it. Like several other devices, the Power-Jelq warns that "the biggest mistake that beginners make is to try to force penile gains quickly by overexercising and by doing the exercises too hard."

The advertisements for the Power-Jelq speak very well of it. "I've only been jelqing for one month. In that time I've noticed a significant difference." Not only that, it seems that "jelqing" can bring truly spectacular results. "Currently, many tribes in Africa have similar rituals that young boys perform before moving into manhood. It has been reported that these men have penises that reach 13 inches in length and up to 8 inches in circumference." Presumably, however, the jelqers of tribal Africa do not have the luxury of "sturdy closed-cell polyethylene rollers."

Some men have experimented by hanging weights on their Power-Jelqs, but sadly there is "no specific documentation" for this type of exercise. By the way—hanging weights of any kind from a man's penis is highly inadvisable. If it has any effect at all, it will take years, and it will only stretch it and make it thinner. It could also cause a very nasty groin strain.

The best exercises for your lover's penis are those which you devise yourself, using massage oils or body lotions. As I have said before, the penis is not a muscle, so it will not respond to exercise by increasing in size.

If you really want to try an ancient exercise technique, try this one from Japan. Take two facecloths, one soaking in a bowl of very warm water and the other soaking in a bowl of ice water. Squeeze out the warm cloth and wrap it around your lover's penis, as tight as you can. Leave it for ten seconds, while you swoosh your mouth out with ice water. Then remove it, and immediately take his penis into your mouth. Repeat the procedure with the cold cloth— only this time you should swoosh your mouth out with *warm* water. Repeat five or six times and the circulation in his penis should be tingling!

It's worth mentioning a sexual exercise which will *not* increase the size of your lover's penis but which *can* improve his erections and give him much more intense climaxes. This is the so-called "Kegel exercise" (named after its developer, Dr. Kegel). It simply involves the regular flexing of the pubococcygus (PC) muscle between your lover's legs . . . the muscle which he flexes when he needs to pee but is trying not to. If he has trouble locating his PC muscle, tell him to stop urinating in midflow simply by using his muscles (not his fingers).

The Kegel exercise can be done anywhere—even

sitting at a desk in the middle of a business meeting. All he has to do is contract his PC muscle, hold it for ten seconds, then relax it. He should try to do this at least ten times, several times a day, every day. After three weeks or so, he should begin to notice that his erections are stronger and that his ejaculations are more powerful.

Like all exercise regimes, the Kegel exercise needs time and persistence, but if he does it faithfully, it will eventually give your lover much greater control over his climax.

Gerry, a 33-year-old auto salesman from Gainesville, Florida, said, "My girlfriend Kim put me onto Kegel exercises because she had been doing them for years. She showed me how strong her PC muscle was the very first time we made love, and I could hardly believe it. She can grip my cock with her vagina so that it almost feels like she's squeezing it with her fingers. I don't think my cock is any bigger than average size, but when your girlfriend can grip you like that, it doesn't *need* to be bigger, does it?

"I could see what benefits a woman would get out of Kegel exercises, but I didn't really see what they could do for a man. Still, I said that I'd give them a go, and I did. I was sitting behind a desk all day, so I didn't have anything else to do.

"At first I didn't notice any effect at all, and I nearly gave it up. But one night we went to Kim's sister's birthday party, and Kim had a few drinks and when we came home she was really in the mood for love. She pulled my shirt and my pants off and she started to suck my cock like she wanted to swallow it, and rub it with her hand. She didn't give me head very often so I was very turned on. It didn't take long before I could feel myself coming, even though I didn't want to come so soon. But, do you know, I squeezed my PC muscle—not consciously, by any means—and I held it tight for ten seconds or so, the same way I do when I exercise, and I stopped myself from climaxing, like I'd jammed on the brakes.

"I was able to roll over and pull down Kim's panties and put my cock inside her, and give her a long, slow fuck. She loved it, and she was giving me that PC squeeze herself, which is almost like having your cock milked. But when *she* squeezed, *I* squeezed too, and held it for a count of ten, and I was able to stop myself from climaxing four or five times.

"When I did come, it was like nothing I'd ever experienced before. My muscles were clenched up tight, and then suddenly they went into spasm and I couldn't stop them, and it was like my whole soul was shooting out of my cock. Kim and me, we were clinging onto each other and it was one of those moments when you don't know where one person ends and the other begins. So if anybody ever asks me about Kegel exercises, all I say to them is, do you want to find out what fucking your partner is *really* all about? Because this will change your life."

I asked Gerry and more than one hundred other men from different walks of life what they thought about the prospect of having a bigger penis. They all agreed that it would be great if exercises and penis-enlargement pills really worked, but ninety-six of them volunteered the opinion that "what you do with it" is much more important than size.

Surgical enlargement: is the only sure-fire method of permanently adding length and or thickness to a man's penis. Some men are referred for surgery because they have so-called micropenises, and they need extra inches to have anything like a normal sex life . . . but thankfully this condition is extremely rare.

Most men who seek surgical enlargement have perfectly serviceable penises. They simply *think* that they aren't big enough. For one reason or another they are usually suffering from very low self-esteem, and their penis becomes the scapegoat for all of their day-to-day problems, especially their status at work and their relationships with women.

Like women who feel that they need breast enlargements, they often believe that if only they had a bigger penis, all of their problems would be solved. Men would look at them with greater respect and women would gasp in admiration.

Some men want bigger penises for the sake of vanity. A good proportion of men who seek surgical penis enlargement are bodybuilders. As we have discussed, the penis is the only part of a man's body which he can't effectively increase with exercise, and many bodybuilders think that a regular-sized penis looks ludicrously tiny in comparison to their outsize muscles.

One well-known penis-enlargement surgeon showed me photographs of a bodybuilding client whose penis is now so thick that he is unable to close his hand around it, and another whose penis is so long that it almost reaches his knees.

So will a surgically augmented penis really solve all a man's problems? Studies have shown that a substantial number of women who have breast enlargements feel more confident and more attractive after their operations. Unfortunately there is no objective research on the satisfaction levels of men who have had penis enlargements, apart from what their own doctors have reported, and they are obviously biased.

Of course all of us men would feel ten times more virile if we had giant penises bulging in our pants, but apart from bolstering our confidence, is penis enlargement really necessary? Does it make a man a better lover? Does it make him more attractive to women?

Length? A woman's orgasm is not dependent in any way on deep penetration, and most women find that a penis longer than eight inches can be positively uncomfortable, especially if it's rammed right in.

Girth? A woman's vagina is extremely elastic, and even though many women say that they like a nice thick penis, an average-sized erection is more than enough to give them that "filled-up" feeling.

It's *stimulation*, not size, that makes a terrific lover. During intercourse, a woman's perception of the size of her lover's penis is affected far more by the height of her sexual excitement than it is by its actual dimensions. Over the years I have talked to hundreds of women about their sexual experiences, and in almost every case they swore that the men who aroused them the most had the largest penises. By the law of averages, this couldn't be true. The simple fact is that the men who aroused them the most *felt* larger.

There are several different surgical procedures involved in penis enlargement. To *lengthen* the penis, the surgeon will cut the suspensory ligaments that connect the penis to the pubic bone, and tug the penis forward. There is almost as much penile shaft inside a man's body as there is outside, and what the surgeon will do is pull at least 30 percent of it out. He will then cover the exposed ligament with skin flaps, which are also supposed to keep the penis stable when it gets erect.

To *thicken* the penis, the surgeon will harvest fat from the lower abdomen or the upper thigh and insert it under the skin of the penis, rather like pushing chestnut stuffing under the skin of a chicken. He might alternatively use fat that he has removed from the patient's body by liposuction, or a tissue product called AlloDerm.

The surgeon can make the penis *look* longer by using liposuction to remove the pad of suprapubic fat just above the base of the penis. In plumper patients, this can visually add almost an inch. Sometimes a patient will have a "turkey neck"—a web of skin that connects the scrotum to the underside of the penis—and the penis can be made to look longer by cutting this back.

Most surgeons recommend postoperative stretching exercises or vacuum pumping.

Average gains in length: about 1 inch. Average gains in thickness: about 1½ inches. Average cost of penile lengthening (with or without girth enhancement): five thousand dollars. Average cost of thickening penis with dermal fat grafts when performed as an independent procedure: about six thousand dollars.

This book is intended to give you positive ways of getting the best out of your partner's penis, and so I am not going to dwell on the case histories of penis enlargements that went wrong. I presume that many men must be satisfied with their longer penises, because the penis doctors are still in business and flourishing. As with all surgical procedures, however, there is always a risk of error or infection. New Jersey urologist Malcolm Schwartz said, "There's a price to be paid. The lengthened penis, when erect, is likely to point straight downward, aiming at the feet."

There have also been cases of bleeding, tissue rejection and the formation of lumpy, unsightly scar tissue—not to mention "pain that went way beyond *any* pain that I have ever experienced."

I strongly feel that there is insufficient scientific research into the current techniques of penis enlargement, and that your partner's penis is too delicate and too complicated for him to allow a surgeon to halfway cut it off, all for the sake of an extra inch. Your lover may be deeply depressed that his penis isn't very big, but there are plenty of ways that you can show him that it is more than big enough for you.

Penis enlargement can only be measured in inches, but the sexual fulfillment that you can help your partner to find inside his mind is *infinite*.

Four: At Long Last Love

How to Keep Your Lover Up All Night

It is hard to credit it now, but before Masters and Johnson published *Human Sexual Response* in 1966, there was hardly any open discussion of the fact that it usually takes longer for a woman to reach an orgasm than a man.

Dr. William H. Masters and Virginia E. Johnson carried out a controversial sex research program in St. Louis, Missouri, using live men and women to study sexual arousal and orgasm. Their book was written in technical language for physicians, but it became a worldwide best-seller, because it showed that female orgasm was not just possible and natural, but highly desirable as the highest form of sexual satisfaction.

In fact, in my early years at *Penthouse* and *Penthouse Forum* magazines, I frequently talked to women in their 30s and 40s who had never had an orgasm and didn't even know what an orgasm was. I shall never forget talking to a woman in her early 50s who had read one of my articles about orgasm and managed to achieve one for the very first time. Her bitterness at "all those lost years" was indescribable.

One of the great breakthroughs that Masters and Johnson made was to show that men and women are sexually aroused in different ways. Men are easily excited by erotic sights and by titillating touching, while a woman's arousal depends very much more on her state of mind and her total feeling of responsiveness toward her partner.

Their most interesting discovery, however, was not how *different* men and women are when they're sexually aroused, but how *alike*.

This led them to argue that the "arousal gap" between men and women isn't a result of physical differences, but of emotional and social conditioning. In other words, women are more cautious about "letting go" than men are, and even flirtatious, promiscuous women are subconsciously looking for signs of sexual commitment.

There have been endless scientific arguments about this, but the fact remains that what happens when your lover and you are both sexually aroused is remarkably similar, except that you tend to reach your climax much more slowly than he does.

Masters and Johnson divided human sexual response into four distinct stages: **excitement, plateau, orgasmic** and **resolution**. Early in the **excitement** stage, your lover's penis becomes erect, while you start to produce vaginal juices which are obviously intended to lubricate your vagina and make it easier for your lover to put his penis inside you. Some women can become juicy in ten seconds from first arousal, so there is not always much of an arousal gap there.

During the **plateau** stage, while your lover's penis is becoming more and more stimulated by oral, vaginal, manual or anal friction, his glans increases in size and grows even more purplish in color. At the same time, your vagina starts to increase both in length and in diameter, and its walls flush darker in the same way as the head of his penis.

Toward the end of the plateau stage, the interior of your vagina around the neck of your womb (your cervix) increases in volume. At the same time, the muscles around your vaginal opening start to clench, which Masters and Johnson called "the orgasmic platform"—the launchpad for your climax.

When your lover reaches the **orgasm** stage, muscular contractions along his penis shoot his semen into your vagina. The first two or three contractions are very powerful and follow each other very quickly, but subsequent contractions are not so strong and come at longer intervals.

As you reach orgasm, you experience strong waves of muscular contraction around the opening of your vagina. The first few waves come once a second, but gradually they subside, and become less regular.

In the **resolution** stage, after his climax, your lover loses his erection, although his penis may not immediately return to its normal flaccid size. Your "orgasmic platform" relaxes and increases in diameter, while the rest of your vagina contracts.

It's not just your sexual organs that behave in very similar ways. In the plateau phase, both you and your lover experience muscular contractions in various parts of your body, especially your face, your hands and your legs. Because of this, you will hold each other very tight, and your teeth will more than likely be clenched. Nobody looks their best in the throes of a climax.

Since "the arousal gap" was first publicly aired, most men have become aware that women usually require lengthier stimulation before they can reach an orgasm, and Masters and Johnson's research did an enormous amount to make them into more considerate lovers. During the course of preparing this book I asked over 100 men if they regularly ensured that their partners reached orgasm when they had sex. Over 73 percent said that they did, while 21 percent said that they "were aware" if their partners hadn't reached an orgasm, and only a few said that they wouldn't know if their partner had reached orgasm or not. "Women always fake it anyhow," said one 45-year-old Philadelphia stockbroker, with complete conviction—so there will always be one or two sexual dinosaurs.

If you are involved in a brief, passionate encounter, it is much less likely that your partner will be specifically concerned about making sure that you reach orgasm, and often the sexual intensity of these affairs makes orgasmic satisfaction less of a priority: it's just the being together that makes it so exciting. But in a long-term relationship, it is vitally important both physically and emotionally for you to have regular climaxes. Women feel extremely frustrated and neglected if their partner never makes a special effort to ensure that they reach orgasm—even if they never have the confidence to come out and say so.

Jodie, a 31-year-old teacher from Madison, Wisconsin, told me that her partner of three and a half years had only once given her an orgasm. "That was after a social function we held at the school. He drank so much punch that he couldn't reach a climax, but he hadn't drunk so much that he couldn't keep his cock up, and he was determined to keep on and on banging away until he got there. At first I was angry, but after about five or ten minutes I began to realize that he was actually doing it for me. I had this amazing feeling rising up between my legs and I felt a tremendous urge to fuck him back. I don't think he knew what had hit him. I rolled him over onto his back and I sat on his cock and I went for it. His cock was so big and hard and it went right up inside me, and I could feel his balls bouncing against my bottom. I galloped up and down on top of him faster and faster and then I couldn't do anything to stop myself. My orgasm shook me like I was a rag doll. I had never screamed in bed before but I did then. Darren was so out of it that I don't think he understood what had happened. It felt wonderful . . . but the sad thing was that it wasn't *us* doing it, or Darren doing it to me . . . it was just me, masturbating, when it came down to it, like I usually do, except that I was using a living cock instead of a vibrator."

Jodie's usual method of reaching orgasm was to masturbate after Darren had gone to sleep, using her fingers or a penis-shaped vibrator. "Maybe it's my fault. Maybe I should explain to him that he's not satisfying me in bed. But that isn't as easy as it sounds. He makes love in the same routine way every single time, and if I told him that I was bored and that I never had an orgasm, I don't think he'd know how to deal with it. I think it might even break us up, and I don't want that to happen. I do love him."

Some men make a genuine effort to bring their partners to orgasm, but always ejaculate too soon. "He has me right on the very edge," explained Sandra, 27, a sales assistant from Chicago, Illinois. "He likes to make love to me from the side, so that he can reach around and play with my clitoris while he's fucking me. So many times I'm nearly there, but the trouble is he becomes aware that I'm nearly there, and that arouses him so much that he climaxes. Then—that's it. He loses interest totally, in a matter of seconds. He can make love to me, climax, and then go back to watching the Blackhawks, without even breaking a sweat. He's a great guy and very sexy, except that he never lasts long enough, and once he's had his climax he doesn't care how I feel at all."

All the same, a number of lovers are much more considerate. If they have climaxed before their partners have reached an orgasm, they will continue to stimulate them with their fingers or tongues until they do.

"To be honest with you, this can be a chore," said Ken, a 33-year-old landscape gardener from Richmond, Virginia. "Once you've shot your load, you lose all of that sexual energy, don't you? All you want to do is lie back and have a cigarette. Instead of that, you have to play with her clitoris until she comes. My present partner, she's a lovely girl, but she can take anything up to twenty minutes to reach an orgasm after I've climaxed, so I'm lying there next to her and my wrist's aching and I may be kissing her and sucking her nipples and telling her how much I love her, but inside of my head I'm willing her to get to that orgasm—*get to that orgasm, will you?*—so that I can have a rest."

Many women find that they can reach an orgasm much more quickly if their partner *licks* their clitoris, because the light, persistent lapping they receive from the tip of a man's tongue is more sensitive and more steadily arousing than being fingered. After your lover has ejaculated, however, and his sexual eagerness has diminished, he may no longer relish the idea of licking a vulva that is flooded with his own sperm.

He could use a vibrator to bring you to orgasm, but only *you* know exactly where you prefer it to be positioned, and at what speed, and whether you like it inserted into your vagina or not, and when, and how fast, and how far.

For these reasons, a truly considerate lover will try to give you an orgasm *before* you start having intercourse. He can do this by fingering you or licking you, or any combination of both. Since he won't have climaxed yet, he will still be bursting with sexual tension, and so he will have all the enthusiasm and the energy it takes to give you the stimulation you need.

If it doesn't occur to him to satisfy you first, you can make sure that he gets the idea by exercising your newfound control over his penis. Start fondling it and sucking it before he gets the chance to penetrate you. There isn't a man in the world who will stop you from giving him oral sex. While you're doing it, make sure that you position yourself in such a way that he would have to be dead from the neck up not to realize that you would like him to return the favor . . . that is, with your legs apart, and close to his face, exposing your vulva.

Kelly, a 26-year-old tour guide from Tucson, Arizona, told me, "When you first recommended that I should form a relationship with my boyfriends' penises like they were separate little guys with minds of their own, I thought that was totally bizarre. But it really works. My love life has never been better, and I don't think that any of my boyfriends have ever been happier, either.

"Since I was sixteen I've had twenty-five boyfriends maybe. I think I'm pretty and I've always liked to party. But I hardly ever had a good sexual relationship with a guy, and I hardly ever had an orgasm—not with a guy, anyhow. I thought maybe it was my fault. I like sex, I've *always* liked sex, and I've never been shy about it, but almost every time it seemed like a disappointment. I always went into a relationship thinking *this is the one, this is going to be terrific*, but I always ended up feeling like I was missing out on something, and I could never understand what it was.

"I met John in a hotel bar in Phoenix, and we

clicked pretty much right away. He took me out to dinner and then he asked me back to his hotel room. He opened a bottle of champagne and kissed me and started to undress me. I undressed him, too, and it wasn't long before we were both naked. His cock was sticking up hard, and I did what you suggested and took hold of it, and rubbed it, and wouldn't let it go.

"He took a condom out of his nightstand and opened the wrapper with his teeth. I said, 'Here, lie down, let me do that.' He lay back on the bed and I kissed his cock and started to talk to it. 'Look at you, you great big brute . . . what am I going to do with you?' I squeezed the shaft of his cock hard and I sucked the end of it. It was a great cock . . . he was blond, and his pubic hair was blond and wavy, and the end of his cock was bright pink, almost like it was modeled out of candy. It tasted good, too. That salty-pickle taste of cock.

"I started to suck his cock up and down, not too hard, and stick the tip of my tongue into the hole. He didn't say one single word. It was like he was in a trance, you know? I fondled his balls, too, and stretched the skin of his ball sack.

"I climbed astride him, with my legs wide apart. He lifted his head up and licked at my pussy. He gave me a few light licks at first, but then he took hold of my thighs and lowered me down so that he could press his face right into it. I could feel that I was getting very wet. He licked my clit and then he opened my pussy with his fingers and stuck his tongue right inside it.

"I kept on sucking him, but real slow and gentle like you told me. All the time he kept on licking me faster and faster and after awhile I couldn't concentrate on sucking his cock any more, I was just holding it in my mouth and panting. I could feel that my pussy was very wet. It was running down my thighs, and I could hear him slurping it, which turned me on even more. Here was this gorgeous guy, and he was drinking the love juice out of my pussy.

"I didn't seriously expect to have an orgasm, but I did, and I went *whoop-whoop-whoop!* and I felt as if every single muscle in my whole body went into a spasm. I had never had an orgasm like that before. It was *sensational*. It was wide-screen. I fell onto the bed and I was shaking . . . and do you know what the great thing was? He fucked me. Turned me over, opened my legs up and fucked me, while I was still jumping and twitching like a cat on a hot tin roof. He pushed this enormous cock right up inside me, as far as it could go, and my pussy was saying *no! yes! no! yes! stop! don't stop!* It was amazing."

Of course the sexual logic in encouraging your partner to give you an orgasm before he penetrates you is obvious. After he has climaxed, a man's penis quickly returns to the state it was in during the early part of the excitement stage—soft and floppy, although it may be slightly larger than its normal everyday non-excited size. Even if he feels ready to have another climax (which he probably doesn't) he will need to go through the whole process of stimulation all over again in order to achieve another erection, and since he has already ejaculated most of his semen, his climax will be nothing so explosive as it was the first time.

You, however, have a tremendous advantage. While you may not reach orgasms as quickly as men, you can go on having one orgasm after another. Provided your lover continues to stimulate you after your orgasm (very tenderly at first, for obvious reasons) your responses will remain at the plateau stage, and very shortly afterward you will be able to achieve another orgasm. And then another, and then another. I have talked to women who have had up to seven "major" orgasms in succession.

The benefits of making sure that you have an orgasm before your lover first penetrates you are:

(a) You are guaranteed satisfaction, even if he ejaculates much sooner than you would like.

(b) Your vagina will be relaxed and very well lubricated, which will lessen the friction on his penis and make it more likely that he will last longer before he climaxes.

(c) Your sexual desire will be less urgent, and you will be able to relish your lovemaking at your leisure.

(d) Your lover will feel that he has already satisfied you, which will enable him to make love to you with more confidence and style and very much less stress. Women in long-term sexual relationships have reported that their lovers tend to display much more sexual skill and variety in their lovemaking if they have managed to give them an orgasm first.

Kelly's success shows how important it is for you to take control of your partner's penis right from the outset. A man's natural instinct is to penetrate your vagina as soon as he can, especially if he's making love to you for the first time. It's a "possession" thing as well as a "reproduction" thing. He doesn't necessarily think that if he hasn't put his penis inside you, he can't cut a notch on his bed headboard. His desire to have intercourse may very well be inspired by affection and respect, as well as physical attraction. But it's natural for him to feel a very strong urge to "own" you. Just think of the words they use in romantic fiction—"He took me," "He possessed me," "He claimed his prize."

Although his urge to penetrate you is so strong, what you want is good sex, and good *long-lasting* sex, and because of the arousal gap, it's important for you to delay penetration for as long as possible. The only way you can do that is to make sure that you're in control of his penis (or Mr. Sausage, or whatever pet name you've decided to give it).

Establishing a special relationship with your lover's penis will enable you to take charge of your sex life without appearing to be bossy and overassertive. You can be soft and warm and submissive to your lover's face, so long as you keep a firm grip on his genitals.

But supposing you *have* kept a firm grip on his genitals, and you've successfully delayed intercourse by sucking his penis and playing with his testicles— what if he doesn't respond? Supposing he simply lies there while you're fellating him and fondling him, enjoying himself, and doesn't give you any stimulation in return?

I was asked this question thirty-five years ago by women who wanted to know how they could encourage their lovers and husbands to give them oral sex. I talked to some of the most celebrated sexual celebrities of the day, including Xaviera Hollander, the "Happy Hooker," Monique von Cleef, the professional dominatrix; and the late Linda Lovelace of *Deep Throat*. Their answer was unanimous. I included their advice in some of my very first manuals on how to drive your man wild in bed, and the positive response that I received from hundreds of women showed how dramatically it worked (although many said that they found the idea "brazen"). It just shows how—sexually—times have changed in a single generation.

These days, of course, many women do it as a matter of course, and it is no longer considered shocking. It still works, though. If you don't do it already, I challenge you to try it today, and show your lover or your husband tonight, and see if it doesn't bring you a satisfying response.

I am referring, of course, to bikini waxing, or pubic shaving, or hair removal with a depilatory cream. As Linda Lovelace remarked, "For neatness, for sweetness, I always say shave, girls, shave!"

Gina, a 26-year-old gym instructor from Orlando, Florida, said that she had always removed her pubic hair since it had first grown, because her mother always did it, and that when she was 19 she had it permanently removed by electrolysis. "Men shave their chins and nobody thinks anything of it, and you don't see women walking around with hair under their arms. It looks clean and neat and every man I have ever dated has absolutely gone crazy for it. Oral sex? You try and stop them!"

Gemma, a 27-year-old manager at a fashion store in Dallas, Texas, said, "I always used to trim my pubic hair because of wearing swimsuits, usually with nail scissors. But then one day my beautician friend Lola was fixing my hair and polishing my nails and waxing my legs and she dared me to go for the whole Brazilian wax. I was a little afraid that it would make me look like a ten-year-old kid, but it doesn't, because a woman's vagina is so much more developed. I think it makes me look more womanly than ever. My boyfriend, Paul, though—he *loved* it. The first night after I had my Brazilian wax, I said, 'I have something to show you,' and I lifted my T-shirt and I wasn't wearing any panties. You should have seen his face: he was like a kid on Christmas Day. He picked me up and carried me into the bedroom and he stripped himself off in five seconds flat. But he didn't fuck me, not right away. He went down on me and he didn't just lick my vagina, he was sucking my pussy lips right into his mouth and rubbing his face all over it. He was so turned on that I could see the juice dripping from the end of his cock. These days, he gives me oral sex almost every time we make love, and he gives me orgasms again and again until he tires me out. Another thing he likes to do now is make love to me, but take his cock out of me before he reaches his climax, and masturbate himself so that his sperm shoots all over my vagina. Then he slowly gives me a sperm massage with his fingers until I have an orgasm. I would say to any woman to have a Brazilian wax. It smarts when you have it done—agreed. But I think it's the single sexiest thing that a woman can do to put a thousand volts into her lover's cock."

Rather like taking charge of your partner's penis, removing your pubic hair makes a silent declaration of sexual compliance. You are exposing your vulva to him, unscreened and unprotected, and encouraging him to look at it and touch it. You are saying to him: "I want you . . . here I am, come and enjoy me." But you don't have to say a word. Dean, 35, an airline pilot from Omaha, Nebraska, said, "I'll tell you what turned me on most of all . . . it was the thought that while I was away flying, Janie was in the bathroom shaving off her pubic hair so that she would be ready to make love to me when I came home."

Of course shaving or Brazilian waxing won't guarantee 110 percent that your partner will give you oral sex before he puts his penis into you, but it will give him the best possible incentive. Many women have said that their partner's obvious excitement at seeing their naked vulvas excited *them*, too, so that they were well lubricated with vaginal juices before they made love.

It isn't *always* necessary for your lover to give you an orgasm first. Some nights, you may not particularly care if you reach an orgasm or not, so long as you have a really good romp in bed. But having an orgasm first is very constructive if you feel in the mood for making love until dawn.

To make love successfully all night, your lover needs to have an erection all night, and you having an orgasm is the first step to keeping him up for hours at a time.

You may have heard of Tantric yoga. This is a Hindu system of meditation dating from the fifth century, in which sexual intercourse is regarded as a cosmic process in which consciousness and creative power are brought together to give a flood of joy throughout body and mind.

Consciousness (*Shiva*) is male, and creative power (*Shakti*) is female. *Shakti* dwells in the form of pent-up energy at the base of the spine (*kundalini*). It is the aim of those who follow Tantric yoga to release this creative energy so that it travels up the spine to unite with *Shiva*, in the brain. The embrace of love between *Shiva* and *Shakti* is represented as the supreme marriage between Being and Becoming, and it is often portrayed as a highly sexual unification.

Followers of Tantric sex have to adopt special physical postures (*asanas*), but it is a very spiritual discipline—not to be confused with the sexual jiggery-pokery in the *Kama Sutra*, or other Asian guides to erotic ecstasy, as arousing as these can be.

I am not trying to teach you Tantric yoga, but there are two important elements in Tantric-type sex which can help you to keep your lover erect for very long periods of time, and intensify your sexual pleasure to the point where you can hardly bear it.

The first is **sexual togetherness**. That is, for you

and your lover to concentrate not just on your own sexual arousal but on each other's feelings, too. Most of us have moments during sex when we feel that we are "one" with our partner, and sometimes we feel that we can hardly tell where our own bodies end and our partner's body begins. But really intimate moments like this tend to be fleeting, and occur mainly when we are close to having a climax. You *can* learn to make them last for hours.

Begin your all-night lovemaking with kisses and caresses to his face, hair, lips, shoulders and body. Keep one hand on his penis, lightly but possessively. Remember that you are in charge of his penis, and you want to make that clear right from the very beginning. He will be kissing and caressing you, too, but don't allow him to maneuver you into a position where he is able to pin you down on the floor or bed or couch or wherever you're making love, and penetrate you with his penis before you have the chance to stop him. You can do this by adopting a half-sitting position next to him, and gently pushing *him* onto his back.

You may feel that you want to have his penis inside you as soon as possible, in which case, what can I say? Go ahead and enjoy it. You can still have a great night of sex ahead of you, even if you will have to organize it differently. If you have intercourse and he climaxes, you will obviously have to wait at least fifteen to twenty minutes before he can manage another erection, and if he's had a tiring day at work he may want some sleep before he tries again.

If his penis wasn't erect when you first undressed,

your kisses and caresses should have stiffened it up. Even if it's still soft, don't worry about it. He obviously needs to relax and unwind, and there is nothing like some gentle, steady cocksucking to help him to put the cares of the day behind him and think about the pleasures of the night ahead.

Turn yourself around so that your feet are facing his head. Kneel next to him and kiss him around the genital area, still loosely holding his penis and very lightly rubbing it up and down with your fingertips. Make some complimentary noises about his penis. "I love your cock . . . it's so big and hard . . . it's enormous." If it *isn't* big and hard yet, just tell him how much you love it. And talk to the penis itself. "Look at you, you'd just love to go up inside me, wouldn't you?"

Take his penis into your mouth and give it some *very* gentle sucking. This will sound even sexier than it really is if you say "Mmmmm" from time to time and make wet, slurping noises. You may genuinely feel like saying "Mmmmm" and making wet, slurping noises, which is terrific. But even if you don't, remember what we discussed earlier . . . that good lovemaking is all about *showing* what you feel as well as feeling it. It's drama, it's communication, it's acting. This doesn't mean that it's insincere, it simply means that you're taking the trouble to let your lover know how excited you are.

So many men have complained to me that their wives and girlfriends "just lie there" when they make love to them, and seem to suffer sex in silence. When I interviewed the women concerned, however, almost all of them said that they really enjoyed sex, and that they couldn't understand why their partners felt that they were simply tolerating it. Well, the reason was that they hardly ever expressed their enjoyment out loud, or showed their partner how aroused they were.

To be fair, many women prefer to enjoy sex in silence, and find it difficult to talk or moan or scream when they're making love. "I always put myself off if I try to say something when I'm having sex," said 34-year-old Tippi, a nurse from Mobile, Alabama. "I once said something like, 'My God, your cock is the same color as my carpet,' and I laughed so much that I almost fell off the bed."

If you find it difficult to come out with whole sentences when you're making love, then a few appreciative kisses and sucking noises are more than enough. And don't forget when you're sucking his penis to make a show of sticking out your tongue and lasciviously licking it so that he can watch you, and of stuffing his testicles into your mouth, and at the same time keeping up that challenging eye contact.

The more clearly you show him that you're becoming sexually aroused, the more likely he is to want to arouse you even further—by giving you cunnilingus or massaging you with his fingers.

In the very early stages of your long night of loving, make sure that while you are giving his penis your constant attention, you aren't tempted to rub him and suck him so fiercely that he climaxes.

Try to relax. Think of his penis as a way of connecting with his consciousness. It will help if you try to visualize the sexual pleasure inside of your own head as a warm, dark ball of fluid, like oil floating in water. Imagine that this ball of pleasure is entering your mouth and enrobing the head of his penis. From there, it pours *up* his penis, in between his legs, and there it meets his own ball of pleasure, which has descended down his spine from his brain. *Your* pleasure and *his* pleasure meet together and combine to form one fluid ball of togetherness—and this combining together is so sexually thrilling that you can hardly believe that such a sensation is possible. It isn't just a physical sensation, it's not just nerve endings. It's a state of mind as well. Sheer erotic bliss. And you haven't even had intercourse yet.

So few couples manage this kind of sexual unification, yet it isn't at all difficult to achieve, and it can bring you to the very highest levels of satisfaction. It can make your mind curl as well as your toes. You need to be calm, and to concentrate your mind, and more than anything else you need to be *generous,* and to teach your partner to be equally generous in return. This is why I place such emphasis on your constant devoted pampering of your partner's penis, and which is why I suggest that you put yourself into sexually provocative positions when you begin to make love so that you encourage him to give *you* pleasure in return.

You've met them yourself, haven't you? People who are nice enough people, but who never take the trouble to pay anybody else a compliment, because it simply doesn't occur to them. People who never spontaneously *give* anything—not because they're mean or unpleasant but because they simply don't see the point. But if you show them *how* to be generous, and how much pleasure their generosity can give to other people, they usually learn very quickly.

We're all taught about sex at school, and maybe our parents have had a stab at it, too. We're all told that we have a right to a satisfying sex life, but how rarely we're told that a really satisfying sex life comes from doing everything we can to satisfy somebody else. That's why this sexual togetherness regime is so successful. It says, "Devote yourself to your partner's enjoyment and your partner's needs, and show him clearly how he can do the same for you." When you're sucking his penis, for example, try to think of the thrilling physical sensation that you're giving him, and how proud and aroused he is to see your lips enclosed around his glans. At the same time, don't let him ignore the fact that *you* would like some stimulation in return.

Simone, a 29-year-old legal secretary from Toronto, Canada, said, "I think the trouble is that men don't always know what it is that a woman really wants in bed, and women never tell them. They would rather sleep with them and then complain about them behind their back. Why don't women say, 'You're going too fast,' which is the usual problem, or 'Touch me there,' or something like, 'Do you know what *really* turns me on?' Do you know what gets me going? I love to lie back with my legs wide open while a man takes his cock in his hand and rubs it up and down my slit. I love watching the way my lips cling to the head of his cock, and the way his cock slides against my clitoris. And if you look at the man's face while he's doing this, he's looking down at my cunt, and he's devoting everything to giving me pleasure, and of course he's enjoying it, too. But there's always this kind of tension, because he'd love to push his cock inside me, and fuck me, but he knows that I'm really enjoying this, and he doesn't want to spoil the moment."

This brings us neatly to the second element that we can borrow from Tantric sex, and that is **continence**. As we discussed earlier, men are naturally driven to put their penis into you as soon as possible and ejaculate as soon as possible. Followers of Tantra, however, believe that semen is power, and that the loss of semen is the loss of power.

Hatha Yoga Pradipika says, "Exposure to sexual stimulation arouses this power. Controlled, the power is like steam in a boiler, no longer random."

You and your partner can have an almost endless night of love if he doesn't ejaculate. Not until you both decide that you're satisfied, anyhow.

If you suggest to most men that they have intercourse without reaching a climax, they will probably ask you why they should bother to have intercourse at all. But the benefits of Tantric-style self-control can be absolutely remarkable. A man who manages to control himself and hold back his climax time after time will find that he can keep his erection for hours at a time, and that even when he loses his erection he can soon get it back again, as hard as before, or even harder.

Once your lover has accepted the idea that intercourse doesn't inevitably have to lead to his having a climax, and that he can keep his erection almost indefinitely if he holds himself back, you won't believe how skillful and subtle he can be when he makes love to you . . . and *he* won't believe how good he is, either. Trying to hold back his climax will slow him down, which will be very much to your advantage. He will also pay more attention to arousing you by other means apart from his penis—playing with your breasts and your clitoris, and kissing you.

At first, most men find that Tantric-style continence leaves them feeling highly frustrated. But that's only because they have *always* had intercourse with the aim of ejaculating, and if they don't ejaculate, they don't feel as if they've "done it." More importantly, they haven't yet learned to concentrate their minds and focus their sexual feelings, and so they don't yet realize how much pleasure they're going to get out of it. It's the difference between swilling down a glass of vintage wine while you're talking and laughing and eating cheese straws, and sipping it slowly, and smelling its nose, and letting it glide slowly down your throat.

We will see later that many men suffer from erection problems precisely because they don't concentrate when they make love, like people who drink wine without actually tasting it. Their brains are scattered all over the place. Sometimes, while they're having intercourse, they're still thinking about work. Or taking their automobile into the shop for a service. Or their partner's hairstyle. Or the mole on her shoulder. And suddenly their erection is dying away and they don't know why.

When your lover learns to hold himself back, however, he will discover that he can stay harder for very much longer, and that the pleasure he can feel in his penis is absolutely amazing. Neil, a 37-year-old engineer from Houston, Texas, e-mailed me simply to say, "It's like discovering sex for the very first time. I love it. It feels so erotic sometimes that I have to bite my lip. These days I can get wood just by thinking about taking my wife to bed, and we've been married for eleven years."

Sexually, your lover will start to feel like a completely different man—more potent, more virile, more energetic. He will be better at sex and much more interested in sex—but not like an adolescent. Once he has learned how to hold back his climaxes, he will be much more mature in his lovemaking and much more capable of controlling his passion.

A considerable number of men have told me that controlling their climaxes has had a beneficial effect on their lives *outside* of the bedroom, too. Gerry, a 33-year-old surveyor from Seattle, Washington, said, "I was always good at my job but I admit that I was not very focused. I had a short attention span—starting one project and then dropping it and picking up another. After I started to train myself to hold back my climaxes, I gradually found that my general concentration improved, and that I was able to devote my attention to a single project and carry it all the way through to the end, without letting anything else distract me. I felt physically and mentally stronger, although that could have had a lot to do with the fact that my sex life was so much more exciting.''

Followers of Tantric yoga believe that a man's mental and physical strength is contained in his *bindu*, his semen, and that every time he ejaculates he becomes a little weaker. There is no medical evidence for this, but I do firmly believe that exercising mental control over any physical function is good for you—especially sex, which involves both voluntary and involuntary actions, as well as emotional responses.

Your partner's penis is not a muscle, and so it isn't possible for him to make it more powerful with *physical* exercise, but he can improve his *mental* control over it, and that will make it harder for longer, which is all that he needs to make him a much more satisfying (and a much more satisfied) lover.

So how do you go about helping your partner to control his climaxes?

If possible, you should explain to him what you're trying to do, and enlist his active cooperation. After all, he's going to get just as much pleasure out of this as you are. If he's not the kind of man who finds it easy to talk about sex—or if he's cautious and conservative in bed—you'll just have to introduce as much of this technique into your lovemaking as you can, so that he gradually becomes aware that your sex life is getting more exciting, and becomes a willing participant.

Prepare your bedroom for your all-night loving session by making sure that it is warm and comfortable and that you have everything you need, such as wine or soft drinks and any massage oils or sexual lubricants or condoms or sex aids. Candles are clichéd but they are always romantic, especially scented candles, and music can be very conducive to love-making provided you don't have to keep getting up to change the CD or skip a couple of tracks that you don't particularly like.

First of all—as we have already discussed—you should encourage your lover to give you an orgasm *before* he puts his penis inside you. To be realistic, you may not physically be able to deter him from initiating intercourse, or you may not be able to make him understand that you would like him to bring you to orgasm before he penetrates you (yes—there will always be men who don't understand what you want in bed, even if you explain it in words of one syllable).

If he *does* insist on having intercourse with you before he gives you an orgasm, he is far more likely to reach a climax before you do, for the reasons we have talked about (more physical friction, more sexual tension). But if he can't stop himself from penetrating you and having a climax, don't despair—enjoy it. After he has ejaculated, you will just have to wait a half hour or so while he recovers his strength before carrying on. You don't have to get up and do the ironing, though. During this "refractory" or resting period, even if he is dozy and reluctant, you can guide his hand between your legs so that he can play with your clitoris and keep you up on the plateau stage of stimulation. As he gradually regains his sexual enthusiasm, he may even be able to give you an orgasm with his fingers or his tongue before his erection returns and before he is ready to put his penis inside you for a second time. That would take a lot of the anxiety out of your lovemaking, since he wouldn't then feel that he *had* to satisfy you as a matter of urgency.

Let's suppose that he *has* given you a prepenetration orgasm. If he isn't lying on his back already, make sure that he lies on his back now, his head supported by a pillow so that he can see what's going on. If his penis is erect, take hold of it and insert it slowly into your vagina, as far as it will go. If it isn't yet erect, you can rub it with your hand or suck it until it stiffens, and then insert it. Don't worry if it takes some time to become erect, especially if he has already had a climax. The thing to remember about making love all night is that you've got all night, so you're not racing against the clock.

You may find that his penis grows stiffer quicker if you start "talking dirty" to him. As we have seen, many women prefer to make love in silence, and are easily put off by conversation during sex. But during foreplay, suggestive murmurings can be highly stimulating, particularly if you can find a fantasy that really flicks your lover's sexual switches. Dirty talk may distract you when you are having intercourse, and you're very close to an orgasm, and your concentration is intense. But when you're simply lying by your lover's side, and you're both relaxed, and you're fondling his penis to make it erect—that's a very good time to try it out. If it puts you off, or it makes you laugh, then it really doesn't matter. There's no law against laughing while you're making love—in fact, some couples ought to try it more often.

When you're talking dirty, try to think of some of the most extreme male sexual fantasies that you can. You will be surprised how quickly you find out which fantasies turn him on and which don't, because you'll be holding a highly sensitive barometer in your hand—his penis. Clare, 31, a restaurant manager from Baltimore, Maryland, said, "My husband Freddie was lying beside me trying to sleep but I felt like making love and so I started playing with his cock and whispering things in his ear. I said stuff like, 'Wouldn't you like to put your cock inside me?' and 'How would you like me to suck it and swallow your sperm . . . I could do that for you.' I began to get a few twitches out of his cock, even though he was still determined to go to sleep. Then I said, 'Do you know what I'd really like . . . I'd like you to push your cock up my ass. I've always wondered what that would be like.' Well—I had never seen his cock go up like that before. It was like a space shuttle. He opened his eyes and looked at me and said, 'Do you really mean that?' and I said, 'Sure . . . we've never done it before, let's see what the big deal is.' Believe me, that started a night like I've never had in my life. Freddie went to the bathroom and came back with a tube of KY and his cock was still sticking up hard. He was good, though—very loving, very tender. He didn't just stick it in. He kissed me and played with my nipples, because he knows how much I like him to play with my nipples. I think I must have oversensitive nipples. I took hold of his cock and it was so hard. I rubbed my thumb around the opening and it was slippery and so I could tell how much he wanted me.

"I climbed onto my hands and knees and Freddie knelt behind me. He smothered his cock in KY, and my asshole, too, sliding his finger in and out of it a few times to relax me. He'd done *that* before, but never with his his cock. Then I felt the head of his cock against my asshole, and he pushed. At first my whole instinct was to tighten up, and he couldn't even get it in an inch. But then I realized that I needed to open up, and so I pushed against him, and the next thing I knew his cock was slowly sliding up inside my bottom. He got it all the way in, right up to his balls. I reached around with my hand and I could feel how much he had stretched my asshole open.

"He didn't move . . . he just kept it inside me, and I squeezed the muscles in my ass so that he could feel me. Then he eased himself sideways onto the bed, without taking his cock out of my ass, so that we were lying side by side. He started to massage my clitoris with one hand, and to fondle my pussy with the other. My pussy was so wet and juicy, and he smeared it all around my thighs and over his balls. It's hard to describe what it felt like having that huge hard cock up my ass. It was partly painful but much more exciting than anything I'd ever felt before. It was even more exciting because it was Freddie's secret fantasy, something he'd always wanted to do but never had the nerve to ask me, and I was doing it for him."

One New York woman told me that she had discovered her partner's penchant for sex in dangerous places by "talking dirty" to him one evening while she fondled his penis. He "noticeably stiffened" when she suggested that they make love in toilets and art galleries. After that, she came on to him several times in elevators, at dinner parties, and (twice) in the Guggenheim. "So far we've been caught only once, in the men's room outside the Oyster Bar in the Plaza. I accidentally kicked my thong under the door, and when I opened the door to retrieve it, there was the washroom attendant, and he didn't look too happy. Well, I was naked from my necklace down."

Your newfound familiarity with your partner's penis should help you, too, to find out his favorite sexual fantasies. Many men will *hotly* deny that they are aroused by certain sexual fantasies, especially those fantasies which turn them on the most. "Would you like to see your girlfriend peeing?" "Of course not! What kind of a man do you think I am?" This is because they are too embarrassed to admit that they could be turned on by sexually incorrect scenarios such as girls having sex with other girls, or ejaculating on a girl's face, or watching women having sex with dogs or horses. Remember this, though: a man's sexual fantasies don't reflect his true personality, or even his true sexual inclinations. All of us can conjure up pictures of extreme sexual scenarios when we're highly aroused . . . scenarios that we might normally find unexciting or even distasteful. The most sexually balanced man can be aroused by fantasies of forcing a woman to have sex, or being whipped and sexually abused, but that doesn't mean for a moment that he needs to do it for real, or that he would actually enjoy it if he did. Fantasies are exactly that—*fantasies*. Clare discovered one fantasy that her husband *did* want to do for real, and which they both enjoyed. But the point is that even if you *don't* act them out (and you usually won't) you can use your knowledge of your lover's fantasies to trigger off a very strong sexual response, whenever you want to.

What if your lover won't admit to having fantasies? Or if he will—what if he won't tell you what they are? Or what if you think that he's censoring his fantasies, and only telling you about the clean ones, or the ones that involve you, darling? Don't worry—if *he* won't tell you, his penis almost certainly will. It's remarkable how much a man's penis swells when he is highly stimulated by an erotic fantasy, even if he is already erect. But what should you do, when you talk about a particular sexual act—say, threesomes—and you feel that telltale extra stiffening? My advice is: don't say anything, unless you're trying to masturbate him toward a climax. Bookmark it for the future. One night you can whisper some erotic suggestions about "threesomes" into his ear, and what you whisper into his ear is very likely to elicit an immediate response from between his legs.

So . . . the music is playing, the scented candles are flickering. Your lover is fully erect and his penis is inside you, and you are sitting triumphantly on top of him. How can you teach him to delay his climax?

Thirteen Steps to Keep Your Lover Up All Night

1) **Taking Him In.** Sit on top of him, with his erect penis fully inserted in your vagina, but *don't* move up and down. In sexual therapy, this is known as "vaginal containment." Stimulate him only with rhythmic contractions of your PC muscle (see those Kegel exercises, earlier!). If you wish, you can stimulate yourself by gently stroking your clitoris, and make sure that he can clearly see what you're doing. You will not only arouse him visually, you will teach him exactly how you prefer to be fingered.

2) **Visualizing His Penis.** Mentally focus on his penis inside your vagina, and try not to let yourself be distracted by anything else. Imagine the interior of your vagina, enclosing his penis. Dark, warm, resilient and welcoming. With each muscular contraction, try to imagine that you're squeezing all the pleasure that *you* can feel into his penis. Hold each squeeze for as long as you can, and try to feel the *shape* of his penis—the glans, the corona and the shaft. Your vagina has molded itself into this same shape.

3) **Sensual Transference.** Stay on top of him for at least fifty unhurried squeezes, and make each squeeze longer and stronger than the last. Once you have become fully conscious of the shape of his penis, try to imagine what *he* can

feel . . . the warmth and juiciness of your vagina, and the gentle rhythmic massage as your
muscles contract. Imagine what it's like to
penetrate another human body. With each of
these fifty squeezes, try to think less and less
of your own sensations and more and more
of *his*.

4) **Mutual Arousal.** Resist any effort he may
make to start thrusting his penis in and out of
you. Tell him instead to start flexing his PC
muscle, in time with yours. You may wish to
count each squeeze out loud together—"one,
two, three, four, five, six, *relax*"—and this can
be very erotic indeed, because you are sharing
a strong sexual sensation in unison. You can
hold hands while you are doing this, which
adds to the feeling of togetherness.

5) **Bringing Him Back from the Brink.** If he feels
that he is coming too close to a climax, you
should both stop squeezing your PC muscles
for a while, and relax. He can keep his penis
inside your vagina unless he warns you that,
if he doesn't take it out, he won't be able to
stop himself from ejaculating. Some couples
agree on a prearranged signal to indicate that
the man is right on the brink of ejaculation,
such as three quick thumb-presses in the palm
of the hand—or he can simply say "Stop!
I'm coming!"

6) **The Pressure Point.** If he's coming too close
to climaxing, take his penis out of you and
apply the "squeeze technique" described ear-

lier in this book—with the ball of your thumb pressing on the top of his glans and two fingers just below the urethra. Squeeze hard until he assures you that the feeling has passed. You can use this squeeze technique as many times as you like to postpone his climax.

7) **Changing Position.** Now he should lie on his side, while you should lie on your back next to him, with one leg over his thigh. In this position he can comfortably insert his penis into your vagina, and at the same time fondle your breasts and your wide-open vulva with his fingers. Again, he should insert his penis into your vagina as deeply as he can, but he should keep it completely still, and resist the temptation to thrust.

8) **The Spiritual Connection.** At first it will take a great deal of self-discipline for your lover to keep himself absolutely still, but he needs to stop thinking about sex as a three-legged race with a climax as the winning post. For too many couples—even couples who love each other intensely—having sex amounts to little more than a rapid bout of mutual masturbation. When it comes to intercourse, they each retreat within their own thoughts and their own sensations, and they forget that they are supposed to be connecting with another human being. Sex is not only physical but *spiritual*. It's a joining together of minds as well as bodies, and once you and your lover have learned to achieve that kind of unification, you

will be capable of experiencing erotic sensations of such sweet intensity that you will wonder how your nerve endings can stand it. I know this sounds as if I've been smoking something, but it is actually based on sound psychosexual techniques which have been clinically proven to work.

When they first get together, most people have explosive sex. After their first infatuation begins to cool off, however, many couples gradually lose interest in each other because their lovemaking is only physical. Like jogging, or push-ups, or any other activity that has no emotional or spiritual dimension, sex starts to become repetitive and boring, and never seems to take them anywhere. They might seek added excitement in sexy underwear, or sex aids, or unusual sexual activities, or group sex, but while these might temporarily add a little more spice to their sex lives, they are only superficial thrills, and they fail to address the underlying problem. Ultimately—without a spiritual element—the physical side of making love has very little purpose except for a regular release of physical tension.

As soon as you start concentrating on *becoming* each other, body and soul, the purpose becomes totally clear. Animals can copulate, but only humans can join their psyches together when they make love. Your lover's erect penis is so important because it is through this physical connection that you can train your minds to meet together, and the two of you can become one.

9) **The Generous Orgasm.** While he is lying on his side with his penis inside you, your lover should start to stimulate you by stroking your clitoris very gently with his fingertip. At the same time you can reach down and caress his hand, and also open the lips of your vulva wider with your fingertips, so that he feels that you are participating in what he is doing, and that you are opening yourself up to him. You can also run your fingertips around the shaft of his penis where it is imbedded in your vagina, and fondle his scrotum. Keep all of your attention on your genitals, and the place where you physically join, but focus on his feelings, and who he is, and how much pleasure you want to give him. He should carry on stroking your clitoris until he brings you to orgasm, and then another orgasm, if he can. Even when you are having a climax, he should try to keep his penis perfectly still, so that he can feel every single spasm of your vaginal muscles, and so that he can share your pleasure from inside your body. You see what I mean about generosity? In sex, it always brings its own reward.

10) **A Moment's Calm.** After you have reached your second and third orgasms, you should give your lover a few minutes of caressing, all over. Let him lie back while you kiss his hair, his eyes and his lips. Sit astride his face so

that he can taste the juice in your vagina, then kiss and stroke him all over, with lightly trailing fingers. His penis may still be hard, or maybe not, but in either case kiss and caress it, and take it into your mouth. Suck it extremely lightly, so that you don't overstimulate it, but make sure that you gradually bring it back to full erection.

11) **Deep Meditation.** In the next stage, your lover should insert his penis into your anus. (If you don't enjoy anal intercourse, however, he can always insert it into your vagina instead.) Your anus will grip him very tightly, which will make it more difficult for him to move his penis up and down, but at the same time you will both have the shared sensation that he has penetrated you very deeply and very privately. Your lover should sit on the floor with his knees apart. You should then roll a condom onto his penis and lubricate it liberally with KY or any other water-based sexual lubricant. Then lubricate your own anus and rectum as deeply as your finger can probe. With your back to him, slowly and carefully sit on his erect penis until it is fully inserted in your rectum. He should put his arms around you and hold you close, but he should remain still, and not attempt any thrusting. This stage of your all-night lovemaking can be very meditative. It helps if the lights are low, and the music is very soothing, and you have a mirror in front of you, so that you can look

into each other's eyes but also see each other joined as one. After a while you should both close your eyes and concentrate on the feeling of his penis inside you. Squeeze your rectal muscles so that he has to push against you to keep his penis inside your bottom (or do the same with your vaginal muscles). Describe to each other, out loud, what you are physically feeling. Then both of you should try to imagine that fluid darkness in your mind, sinking slowly down your spines to join together where you physically join. Let your darkness join with his. Hold that togetherness in your minds for as long as you can.

12) **Controlled Orgasm.** Still sitting in the same position, your lover should start to fondle the lips of your vulva, gently rolling them between his fingers, and stroke your clitoris, gradually bringing you to yet another orgasm. Resist your orgasm for as long as you can, to build up its energy, but when it eventually overwhelms you, you should expel all the air from your lungs as forcefully as you can. Shout if you have to, or scream. At the same time concentrate all of your muscle spasms into your vagina and your rectum, and into gripping your lover's penis, so that he can share the full force of your climax. For his part, he should be holding you down, to make sure that his penis isn't wholly or partly forced out of your anus. (The expulsion of air will

help to increase the dynamic of your orgasm, in the same way that kung fu fighters can increase the energy of their blows by shouting when they strike their opponent.)

13) **Encore or Climax.** After this orgasm, your lover should withdraw his penis from your anus and remove his condom. (If you are quite confident about his medical history, he doesn't necessarily have to use a condom, but it would be advisable to wash his penis after anal sex, and going to the bathroom could well interrupt your mood.) You should both make yourselves comfortable on a bed, or futon, or cushions on the floor. You now have a choice, depending on how much energy you both have left. Either he can lie back while you climb on top of him again, and insert his penis into your vagina, and repeat Steps One through Thirteen, or else *you* lie back and allow him to make love to you until he climaxes. If you decide to do this, you should focus all of your feelings on his penis, and try to imagine the increasing pleasure that he can feel in his glans. You might want to caress his testicles as his climax approaches, so that you can feel them rising close to his body, and his scrotum tightening up. When he climaxes, hold him very tight, and concentrate your attention on every quiver of his ejaculating penis. After controlling his climax for so long, the force of his ejaculation should be very

forceful and quite dramatic. On the other hand, he may choose to relax completely, and rest for a while, delaying his climax until later.

The more often your lover resists the urge to climax, the greater control he will be able to exert over his penis during lovemaking. He will soon be able to give you hours more pleasure and many more orgasms, and he will be more than compensated by the pleasure that *he* enjoys, even without ejaculating, and the geyserlike sensation of a climax that he might have postponed six or seven times, or even more. When he first starts to suppress his climaxes, he may well suffer some of that "blue balls" feeling. But he will quickly realize that a few minutes of calm and relaxation can ease that frustration, especially if you are gently fondling his penis and giving him the promise of more excitement to come.

Rick, 28, a software salesman from Detroit, Michigan, said, "I liked to think of myself as a real stallion, but after I tried this holding-back technique I realized that all this time I was just a beginner. If I lasted for fifteen or twenty minutes I thought I was really going some, but now I can last for five or six hours, or even more, if I want to.

"If you had told me six months ago that I had to stop myself from coming, I would have said, *Excuse me?* Where's the satisfaction in that? But to give your girlfriend three or four orgasms is amazing. You should see the look in her eyes! For me and Mandy, it's given our relationship a whole new feeling. It's like it used to be when we very first met, when we couldn't get enough of each other and we were fucking every chance we could get.

"But it's better than that. It's like we're very much closer. It's like we can look at each other and understand what the other person is feeling. Mandy and me were making love the other night and I looked up into her eyes and I was sure that I could actually feel what she was feeling. It was like I knew what it was like for her to have my cock inside her, and for one moment I couldn't honestly tell you who was me and who was her. I don't know if you can understand that, but it's like a light going on inside of your head.

"I don't mind not climaxing now. In fact I stop myself coming on purpose. Some nights we fuck for hours and then I go to sleep for a while without even coming at all, although I have to admit that I usually wake Mandy up in the morning and get my rocks off before I go to work. Sometimes Mandy likes to jerk me off. If you've nearly had a climax four or five times, but stopped yourself, you should see it when you finally do. It's like Mount St. Helens, only it's sperm instead of lava. It goes on and on, *pump-pump-pump*, and it feels incredible.

"I know for sure that I'm giving Mandy much more satisfaction and much more loving, and I feel much more of a man. There's a new bond between us, you know? I thought we were in love before but this is different.

"I think that I'm a much more focused person. Much more generous. I can understand now that there's much more satisfaction in *giving* than there is in taking, especially with sex. I also think that I'm much more sexually attractive to women than I used to be before, although right now I'm being faithful to Mandy. It's like having an inner strength. I only have to look at a woman and I know that I could give her orgasms all night, and somehow that confidence *communicates* itself, do you know what I mean? It might sound like I'm boasting, but I think I have sexual charisma."

That was one satisfied customer, but many others have tried the thirteen stages of keeping up all night— or variations of them—with remarkable success.

You and your lover can vary the thirteen stages according to your own particular pleasure, but I recommend that you always try to start off by having an orgasm before your lover puts his penis in you for the first time, and that when he does, you sit on top of him to "contain" his penis and suppress his urge to thrust. After that you can try almost any sexual variation, so long as your lover resists the temptation to ejaculate. Many men find that they can postpone their climaxes while still keeping their erections if they withdraw their penises for a while but keep up the ongoing stimulation by giving their partners oral sex.

Most of all, though, you should both concentrate hard on your mental togetherness. Once you have managed to join your minds as well as your bodies, you will find that your lovemaking is a continuing exploration which can only bring you more and more pleasure and rewards than you ever thought possible.

Five: Rise and Shine

Care and Maintenance of Your Lover's Penis

These days, we don't take our bodies for granted. We eat a balanced diet, we exercise, we drink in moderation and we don't smoke. Well, we do our best, anyway.

Very few men, however, take care of their most important masculine asset, their penis. Yet the penis and its performance is one of the most significant indicators of a man's general health and psychological well-being—quite apart from being his organ of reproduction and his primary method of physical interaction with women.

- Keeping his penis *clean* goes without saying. Or it *would*, if he didn't use urinals, which offer him no means of wiping his penis after he's taken a pee. You wouldn't get up from the toilet without wiping yourself, yet men do it regularly and think nothing of it. Fresh, healthy urine is so sterile that you could drink it without any ill effects, but it's a different story when it's stale.

Would you suck your lover's penis before he took a shower? Would he expect you to? Suggest that he carry a pocket pack of sterile wipes with him, to keep him sweet after he's peed. A man should be ready to make love to you at any time you feel like it. A light touch of anti-perspirant on each side of his scrotum will give him a fresh feeling, too. The singer Tom Jones says that he splashes aftershave on his nether parts, but I can imagine that this might be rather overwhelming (apart from stinging like hell).

- You've already seen how regular fondling can give you an intimate sexual relationship with your lover's penis, but you can also use your fondling to keep his penis in good shape. Next time you manipulate him, smear some moisturizing lotion on the palms of your hands, and rub it into his shaft and his scrotum. You will find that the skin of his penis stays super-smooth, and that his scrotum acquires a texture like crumpled Chinese silk. Choose a mild and lightly scented lotion for his penis, such as Flowers by Kenzo—or for a party night you could use Noa by Cacharel, which contains silver sparkle.

- At least once a week you should rub his shaft really energetically, until it glows. This is unlikely to increase his penis in size, as we have seen, but it is beneficial for his circulation, and it is a good indicator that he can still achieve a rock-solid erection. Erectile dysfunction is one of the first signs that a man is worried, depressed, or that he is suffering from some kind of physical complaint . . . which even *he* may not be aware of.

- Men over 50 and men who are currently without sexual partners should make sure that they vigorously rub their penises at least twice a day. They don't have to climax if they don't want to, but they should make sure that they can readily achieve an erection, and that their erection lasts for a while before subsiding. A penis that never gets any exercise will physically dwindle . . . and, apart from that, it's a good way for a man to check on a twelve-hour basis that he's reasonably fit. (Not only that, it doesn't feel too bad, either.) The very latest research in male sexuality has shown that—contrary to popular opinion—a man's semen doesn't build up if he doesn't have sex. In fact, after only two days it begins to diminish. Dr. Eliahu Levitas at Ben Gurion University in Israel has shown from comprehensive tests that a man who hasn't ejaculated in a long time will have less semen—and be measurably less fertile—than a man who ejaculates regularly.

- Massaging your lover's scrotum with moisturizer gives you an excuse to detect any suspicious lumps. I talked to a senior publishing executive in New York who told me that a masseuse had found a lump in his scrotum during a "relief massage" and probably saved his life. His wife (who was not in the habit of fondling his balls) had never noticed it. A cancerous testicle may become hard, lumpy or swollen. Your lover may complain that it aches or that he can feel a dragging sensation in it. If you find a lump or if you notice any kind of change in your lover's testicles, that doesn't necessarily mean that he has cancer . . . but he should visit his doctor immediately for a checkup. The best time for examining your lover's testicles is after a shower or a bath, when his scrotum is loose. Gently but firmly feel the epididymis on top of each testicle (the spermatic tubes). It should feel soft and tender. Then locate the spermatic cord which goes out from the top of the epididymis and behind the testicle. This should feel like a firm, smooth tube. Finally feel the testicle itself, which should be smooth with no lumps. Lumps are usually found on the front or the sides of the testicles. Of course you can do this examination without your lover even realizing that you are keeping a watch on his sexual health, but it is better if you make him aware of it. Cancer is not the sexiest subject, but there is nothing sexier than caring for the man in your life, and making sure that he lives long enough to give you nights of pleasure for years to come.

- Regularly trim his pubic hair to keep him looking neat and to make oral sex more enjoyable. You don't have to shave him completely (although some women are very turned on by a totally naked penis) but you can remove the stray hairs from his scrotum so that you can take his testicles into your mouth without gag-

ging, and you can cut back excessive under-
growth with electric clippers. Shorter pubic hair
gives the visual impression of a longer penis,
particularly if you completely shave the shaft.
You might even like to try a bit of decorative
topiary . . . arrow-shaped or star-shaped or cut
like a lightning flash. Many naturists and bodybuilders remove all of their pubic hair so that
they are exposing their genitals completely, but
if you are aroused by the all-nude look you
should be warned that it is quite high maintenance. You will need to shave your lover's
pubic area almost every day, making sure that
you use shaving lotion formulated for sensitive
skin, or else you will have to wax it every ten
days or so. Apart from its blatant nakedness,
the main attraction of a hairless cock is the feeling of it when you make love. Both men and
women say that it intensifies a feeling of physical closeness, especially if the woman is hairless,
too. Ray, a 33-year-old musician from Portland,
Oregon, whose wife regularly waxes his penis
for him, described it as "the difference between
swimming in the ocean in your shorts, and
swimming in the ocean stark naked." In Los
Angeles, a specialist in men's grooming told me
that it is becoming increasingly popular for men
to wax the cleft of their buttocks, for a hairless
anus. Prices run about sixty dollars. He said,
"It's cleaner, it's sexier, and it's more civilized.
Most of my clients say that their wives or their
girlfriends asked them to do it. Women are

much more sexually demanding these days, and they know about stimulating their partner's anus with their tongues or their fingers and maybe inserting butt plugs or other sex toys. For that reason they don't want his ass to look like a jungle. I think it's an aesthetic thing, too. It looks more sculptural." Pubic and anal hair can be permanently removed by electrolysis, although this is more expensive and takes much longer. Of course many men are naturally very hairy, and there are plenty of women who love this, too. But there is still no reason why you shouldn't keep his penis and his scrotum reasonably tidy. After all, you wouldn't let him grow his hair on his head like the wild man of Borneo.

• A simple but highly erotic pleasure on a warm day is "penis misting" . . . suffusing your lover's penis and scrotum with a plant-misting spray containing cold water or thin perfumed oil. The sensation is equally erotic when applied to the anus. Another refreshing treatment is to have him kneel down naked in front of a chair with his head and his elbows supported by the seat cushion, and slowly raise a full glass of chilled effervescent springwater to immerse his penis and his scrotum.

Throughout history, and in various civilizations throughout the world, men have decorated and pierced their penises—either to attract attention to them, or to increase their sensitivity, or to give them bumps and lumps which will make them more stimulating for women.

In Varna, Bulgaria, archeologists found a gold ring which was obviously meant to be a penis decoration, and designed to be exposed. It probably dated back to the Copper Age, and may have been used in agricultural fertility rites, with its wearer masturbating onto the fields to make them fertile.

In Borneo, tribesmen decorate their penises with leaves, shells and feathers in order to attract women, and the Dani warriors in the highlands of Irian Jaya in Papua, New Guinea, wear nothing but extremely long gourds on their penises, like surrealistic ice-cream cones. These are especially grown to fit, and their sole purpose is to say "Look what a man I am." When a boy in the Enawene Nawe tribe in central Brazil reaches puberty, his mother ties a thin string of buriti palm leaf around his foreskin and straps his penis back into his body cavity, so that his scrotum bulges out. This is supposed to display his fertility.

Men have had their penises tattooed for centuries, often with birds and animals that appear to grow larger when they have an erection. But probably the most elaborate form of penis decoration is piercing. I was interested to discover during the course of researching this book how many men have some form of genital piercing, and what different walks of life they all came from. They weren't all hippies and bikers, by any means. One of the most complicated penis piercings was worn by a man whom I could only describe as a "captain of industry"—wealthy, influential, and outwardly conservative.

The Dutch dominatrix Monique von Cleef explained to me that some of her most powerful clients often had penis decorations, and that they would frequently ask her to inflict pain on their penises, such as enclosing them in a leather muzzle with needles in it, or strapping them up tightly. She believed that this was almost a tribal assertion of their virility, and very close to some of the rites-of-passage rituals which are still carried out in isolated societies like the Enawene Nawe and the Dayaks.

Inside their pants, when they go to work, they can feel every minute of the day an affirmation of their maleness, and of their dominant position in the world. In a similar way, women who wear rings or studs in their vulvas say that it is not only the decorative aspect of piercing that attracts them, but the twenty-four-hour reminder of their sexuality.

Apart from confirming their virility, men pierce their genitals for a whole variety of other reasons.

- They do it for the *look*, and particularly for the shock value when they display their genitals to their friends or partners. Although it is not as permanent as tattooing, piercing is a very extreme form of genital decoration, and a large part of its erotic attraction is that it involves making holes in a very sensitive and intimate part of the body, which many other people find disturbing.
- They do it because it gives them sexual pleasure, and some piercings are also designed to give added sexual stimulation to their partners—

such as pearls inserted under the skin of the penis.

- They do it as a display of commitment in a sexual relationship, or to show that somebody "owns" them. This might even go so far as to involve a lockable chastity device, to prevent them from having intercourse with anybody else.
- They do it as a rite of passage . . . to mark their eighteenth or their twenty-first birthday, or graduating in the military or other institution, or becoming engaged or married.

The secret knowledge that he is sexually ornamented with rings and studs can give a man sexual pleasure in itself. Many men start with a single ring, but the compelling nature of piercing can lead them to more and more elaborate decoration and more and more holes. Piercing is often combined with an interest in tattoos.

Men can have their penises pierced in several different ways. Some of the piercings date back thousands of years, to ancient Greece and ancient Rome, and Arabia, and the tribes of Southeast Asia— although some were devised much later, like the "dressing ring" which Beau Brummel made popular in Regency England.

One of the most popular piercings is the **palang** or **ampallang,** which was common amongst the Dayak and other tribes in Borneo. The word *palang* is associated with the wooden supports which held up the roofs of their long houses, and so it came to symbol-ize a man's power to protect his family.

The *palang* is like a barbell—a shaft of metal with a blob on each end which goes right through the glans from one side to the other, so that there is a blob protruding on each side. Some piercers insert it so that it goes right through the urethra, while others prefer to insert it more centrally. A *palang*-type bar-bell can also be put through the glans vertically, so that one blob is on top of the glans, and the other protrudes out of the urethral opening. This is called an *apradravya*, and is mentioned in the *Kama Sutra*.

Having a *palang* put in is a very serious piercing, and it can take up to six months for it to heal. Enthu-siasts, however, say that the pain and the hassle and the long wait are more than worth it. "Until you've made love to a woman with a *palang* in your penis, you don't know what sexual sensation is," said Derek, a 36-year-old bookstore manager from New York. "It's so good that when we have intercourse I find myself biting my lips until they bleed, because I don't think I can stand the pleasure. My partner Myra adores it. She just can't get enough of it. Since my piercing healed up, I don't think a single night has gone by when we haven't made love, and that was five and a half months ago. She even wants it during her period. She even calls me at work and says come home because she wants it."

Dydoes are smaller barbells which are worn around the coronal ridge of the penis, to give a crown effect. They are pierced through the corona parallel with the penis, so that the blob at the front gives sexual sensation to the women with whom their wearer is having intercourse, and the blob at the back rubs against the sensitive skin just behind the glans to give sexual sensation to the wearer himself. Some men have their penises adorned with as many as six dydoes, usually arranged in pairs. They are only suitable for men who have been circumcised, and some men who have been circumcised comparatively late in life claim that they bring back the sensitivity that they lost when their foreskin was removed (although sexual sensitivity is almost impossible to measure).

Men with foreskins needn't feel that they're missing out, however, just because they can't comfortably wear dydoes. There are numerous foreskin piercings, including rings and studs, and because the skin is so thin, these piercings heal up very quickly. Foreskin piercings can be a constant source of sexual arousal, since the ornaments are always rubbing against the glans. Twenty-six-year-old Jake, a draftsman from Pittsburgh, Pennsylvania, told me that friction from the tiny metal beads which decorated his foreskin actually caused him to ejaculate in his shorts while he was hurrying to work.

Another sensitive spot which is often pierced is the frenum, the thin web of skin underneath the penis which connects the urethral opening to the shaft. Like foreskin piercings, frenum piercings are relatively painless and they heal quite rapidly. The frenum itself is too thin to be decorated with rings or barbells without tearing, so the jewelry is pierced more deeply into the tissue of the penis. A row of barbells pierced through the frenum is known as a "frenum ladder."

A **guiche** is a ring pierced through the perineum, which is the area in between the scrotum and the anus. *Guiche* wearers often like to hang weights from their rings to give them sexual stimulation whenever they get the chance to walk around naked, and tugging on a man's *guiche* when he is ejaculating is supposed to prolong his climax. However, *guiches* can take a long time to heal, once they're inserted, and they can lead to painful inflammation.

One of the most popular piercings is the "dressing ring" which I mentioned earlier. This was supposed to have been devised by the well-known dandy Beau Brummel in Regency England when it was the fashion for men to wear extremely tight breeches. To keep their penises under control, and to prevent unsightly lumps and bumps, they had a ring pierced through their glans which could be attached to a hook inside one of their trouser legs. Prince Albert is said to have had this piercing done before he married Queen Victoria in 1825, and so it is usually known as a "Prince Albert" or "PA"—so be careful about asking a man where you can get in touch with his personal assistant.

The Prince Albert is a large ring inserted into the underside of the penis just to one side of the frenum, which emerges through the urethra. If your lover feels like trying one, it's worth mentioning that frequent sex can cause wear and tear on a Prince Albert owner's penis, and may lead to him dripping when he urinates, which is not a great turn-on for either of you.

Some men try scrotum piercing or **hafada,** but as you know, the scrotum keeps stretching and contracting according to the ambient temperature, and *hafada* are notoriously difficult to heal. If they accidentally pierce the scrotal sac which contains the testicles, there is a high risk of dangerous infection.

Penis piercing can not only be decorative but extremely erotic, and all of the devotees to whom I talked when I was preparing this book claimed that it had given their sex lives an extraordinary new dimension. Many of them had nipple piercings, too, and said that they had never before realized how sensitive their nipples could be. Several of them said that their partners had decided to have genital piercings, too, including gold rings and diamond studs and *palang*-style barbells through their clitoris.

If your lover wants to pierce his penis, and you like the way it looks and the way it feels, I don't see any reason why you shouldn't go for it. As with any other kind of piercing, however, he should think long and hard before having his penis perforated. It's not the thing to have done at the end of a drunken evening out with the boys. Any infection can be dealt with by removing the offending jewelry and with antibiotics, but there is also the consideration of growing older, which happens to everybody. A senior citizen with barbells in his penis and tattoos all over his body may not look quite as ravishing as he did when he was 25.

I have come across several women whose care and maintenance of their partner's penises have gone way beyond fondling and oral sex and are highly creative. One woman artist in Denver, Colorado, regularly decorates her lover's penis with felt-tip pens, using traditional Native American designs; while an India-born woman in San Francisco, California, embellishes her husband's entire genital area with henna prints. At least one woman from Minneapolis, Minnesota, likes musical accompaniment when she and her partner make love: she ties bells to his scrotum with red silk ribbons—"Every time we make love it reminds me of Christmas."

Some women like to give oral sex a little extra variety. I have come across at least half a dozen women who like to embellish their lovers' penises with frosting and glacé cherries, Hershey's chocolate sauce, butterscotch sauce, maple syrup, and several different flavors of ice cream. They don't always have a sweet tooth, however. Margarita, 31, from New York, once poured warm melted mozzarella cheese on her lover's scrotum and Bolognese sauce on his penis. She even scattered grated Parmesan on his glans.

One of the more amusing penis games is Lingam Gnosis, "the ancient art of penis reading," a light-hearted web site which may nonetheless tempt you to see if you can analyze your lover's character by the appearance of his genitalia. Ms. Yoni Passionata (which, roughly translated, means "passionate pussy") divides penises into four elements—earth, air, fire and water.

Earth penises "resemble tuberous vegetables—yams, potatoes, turnips, etc.," with testicles that are "large, hairy and pendulous." A man with an earth penis is "homely, simple and none too bright," with sexual tastes that are strictly "meat and potatoes."

Air penises are "long, slim and pale, with neat, globular, lightly pigmented testicles." These belong to artistic men who may have bisexual tendencies. Men with air penises are "notoriously fickle," but once captured make imaginative lovers.

A typical fire penis is "thick, straight, symmetrical and smooth" although not too long. It is colored bright red and belongs to a man who is "aggressive, assertive and controlling." Ms. Passionata recommends that if you unzip "one of these crimson lollipops" you promptly zip it up again and move on.

Water penises are "soft, small and feminine in appearance." Their owners are givers and nurturers, and their sense of duty would be almost touching "if it wasn't so irritating." They can sometimes take over the balance of power in a relationship simply by mothering you, and that's when they can become "claustrophobic and scary." However, they can be very sexual, especially when they've had a few drinks.

You can try your own penis readings, just for fun. It's amusing to compare the appearance of your lover's penis with his personality. I don't know if it's possible to tell a man's fortune by looking at his penis, but if it stiffens very quickly while you're doing your reading, then the chances are that his immediate future is going to be very rewarding.

Now to a much more serious side of penis care. We have already discussed penis size, and how seriously some men can be affected by the idea that their penis is smaller than average. This is a self-image problem that can be just as depressing as anorexia or bulimia, or any other chronic lack of personal confidence. It can lead a man to lose his sense of self-assurance in every aspect of his life, both in his career and in his personal relationships.

When a man is convinced that his penis is too small, it is almost impossible to reassure him otherwise. You can quote him all the statistics you like, but it still makes no impression. It can sometimes help to show him naturist magazines containing pictures of men with flaccid penises, so that he can see some photographic evidence that most men have roughly the same size penis as his. But this is rather like showing photographs of normal-sized fashion models to young girls who believe they're too fat. They don't *want* to look normal-sized. They want to look *thin*. And in the same way, men who think their penises are too small don't just want regular-sized johnsons—they want *big* ones.

A man's perception that his virility and his social eminence is somehow related to the size of his penis is a problem in itself. The real problem is someplace else—in his upbringing, in his education, in his relationships with other people, in his own laziness or his own lack of tolerance. But of course it is always easier to blame something or somebody else, and not himself, and men have a sufficiently detached relationship with their penises to be able to point between their legs and say "Blame *him!*" In other words, I'm a big man with big ideas, but through absolutely no fault of my own I was born with this inadequate dinkle.

As we have seen, this penis-blaming is so widespread that literally tens of thousands of men log onto penis-enlargement web sites every week, desperately seeking ways to make their penises bigger and (hence) enhance their standing in the world. Which of course it wouldn't, even if they *could* make their penises bigger. I mean, do they really think that they're going to come rushing into the locker room at the golf club, swinging this enormous python between their legs, and that their whole life is going to be transformed overnight? "Pssst . . . have you seen the size of Merridew's schlong . . . let's promote him to CEO."

All joking aside, however, sexual self-image is extremely important to a man's general well-being, and if he is worried that his penis is too small, he needs to be convinced that it isn't. For this reason I have devised an extraordinary but very effective psychological technique which you can use to change your partner's anxiety about his penis. *Telling* him that his penis is more than big enough is not going to cut it. He needs to *perceive* it, and *believe* it.

An anorexic perceives herself as being much fatter than she really is. To be cured, her perception has to be altered so that she sees herself as being attractive when she is back up to average weight. In the same way, your partner has to accept a new image of his penis, "seeing" it as bigger than it is now. Incidentally, this technique works even if he's not worried about the size of his penis . . . he can still be taught to believe that it's grown.

How to Enlarge His Penis in His Mind

For this technique, you will need only one prop: a giant-sized vibrator or dildo, preferably in the shape of a penis; or, failing that, any cylindrical object such as a pastry pin or a foot-long length of cardboard postal tube, or even a submarine roll.

A vibrator is better because it so closely resembles a human penis, and already has sexual connotations. Vibrators are easily and discreetly available through sex-toy catalogs and are not expensive. Once you have used it for this technique, you can use it for sexual play, too.

If you have the kind of relationship in which you don't have any secrets whatsoever, you can tell your lover that you're trying to make him feel better about the size of his penis. Personally I think that it will be much more effective if he believes—(say) that it's a new way of increasing his sexual responsiveness. That wouldn't be strictly untrue, and he is less likely to feel that you are patronizing him—or that *you*, too, feel that his penis is too small. So much of this technique relies on restoring his self-confidence that you don't want to take two steps back before you've taken even one step forward.

Ask him to undress. You should undress, too, completely or partially. It will help to make his penis stiffen more quickly and more solidly. You should also make it clear that he has to be tested at the end of each session by making love to you. Not only will this lovemaking act as an incentive for him to take part in these "enlargement" sessions, but it will help to make him feel that his virility is improving session by session.

Positioning is important. You can either sit side by side at a dining table, or kneel side by side at a coffee table. Your lover should lean forward slightly with his legs apart so that his stomach is pressing against the edge of the table and he *cannot see his penis*.

Rest the vibrator on top of the table in front of him. Gently run your fingertip down the length of the shaft, and *at exactly the same time*, do the same to his penis under the table. Stroke the vibrator again and again, and simultaneously stroke his penis in the same way. Ask him if he can feel you stroking him, and what it feels like. Ask him if his penis feels as if it's growing bigger. All the time that you are stroking his penis his eyes will be fixed on the vibrator.

Now vary the way you touch the vibrator. You can gently drum your fingertips on it, and tap it, and very lightly tickle the glans with your fingernails. Copy every drum, tap and tickle on his penis under the table. When you're tickling him, ask him again if he can feel it. Ask him if he can feel his penis growing even bigger still, because you can. Tell him that his penis feels almost the same size as the vibrator.

As this technique begins to work, he will begin to

experience the sensory illusion that the feeling in his penis is coming from the vibrator on the table, and that the vibrator is connected to his nerve endings. It's almost unbelievable, but he will perceive this 10-inch plastic penis as being part of *him*. After a while you may even find that you can stroke the vibrator *without* stroking his penis, and yet he can still feel it.

Repeated sessions of about ten to fifteen minutes over a period of two weeks should gradually alter his perception about the size of his penis. He may wonder exactly what you're trying to do, and he may be reluctant to participate every day, but after your lovemaking at the end of each session you can assure him that his sexual sensitivity is improving beyond measure, and that his penis actually feels larger and longer.

Although this technique may seem like a party trick, it's based on serious research that is being carried out at UC San Diego into self-image. If you can persuade your lover to do it regularly, you should notice an improvement in his general assertiveness. Does he talk to other men more directly, and does he look them in the eye? Does he show more confidence with women? Is he more eager in bed, and does he seem more passionate than he did before? All these are signs that you have significantly altered the way his mind sees his penis.

In all, the care and attention that you lavish on your partner's penis will always reward you. His penis will notice, and so will he.

Six: The Harder They Rise

How to Beat Erection Problems

"I thought our sex life was over," said 51-year-old Hannah, a homemaker from Hartford, Connecticut. "Harry retired at the age of fifty-five, and only about three months after he retired, he seemed to lose interest in making love. I tried to talk to him about it but he just got angry and said that everything was fine, when obviously it wasn't.

"He started to drink more, and he started to drink earlier in the day. By the time I went to bed at night he was always asleep, and when I woke up in the morning he was always gone. I had always imagined that when he retired, we would have this idyllic life together, just like it was when we first got married. But it turned into a nightmare. We never had sex, we were always arguing, and I didn't know where to turn."

Hannah wrote to me and I suggested that first of all she should talk to her doctor. Without talking to Harry, it seemed to me that he was probably suffering from psychogenic impotence, which we discussed at the beginning of this book. That is, erectile dysfunction caused by psychological factors.

These psychological factors are many and varied, but the problem is that many men try to keep them bottled up, which only makes them ten times worse. As we have seen, a stressful job is a common cause of temporary ED, and so is divorce, or breaking up with a long-term partner, or financial anxiety, or bereavement. Some men who have a history of unsuccessful relationships suffer from ED, because they have lost all of their sexual confidence, and it can also affect men who are not entirely sure about their sexual identity. They look at another man and find him attractive, but at the same time they feel guilty and ashamed.

You can usually tell if your partner is suffering from psychogenic impotence because he will normally have an erection when he is dreaming and when he wakes up in the morning. This indicates that—physically—everything in the erection department is still in full working order.

Psychogenic impotence tends to come on comparatively quickly, and can usually be directly connected to a time of change or disruption or disappointment in a man's life. In Harry's case, of course, it was his early retirement. Countless men think that retirement is going to be heaven, but suddenly they find that they have no staff to run around after them, no power, no influence, and nothing to occupy their day except cryptic crosswords and golf. Not only that, the "balance of power" in their marriage has changed overnight. They are now spending their days in a

home which has been run for years according to their
wife's regime, and they have to learn to fit in. For
many retired men, this alone is like being emascu-
lated. They wander about all day like lost souls, and
more often than not their wives find it hard to con-
ceal their irritation at their constantly "being there."

Hannah talked to her doctor but Harry refused, so
I talked to him myself. It turned out that soon after
his retirement he had failed to achieve an erection
three times in a week. "I wanted to make love to
Hannah but the old man just wasn't interested. It
seemed like he was even floppier than he is normally,
and even when I rubbed him I couldn't feel him at
all. It was like he was anesthetized."

After his third failure, Harry began to worry that
there was something physically wrong with him. A
friend of his was suffering from ED because of
chronic heart disease. Because of this, he didn't want
to discuss his problem with Hannah, because she
would make him go to the doctor, and he didn't
want to hear the worst. "But it wasn't just that. I
was embarrassed to tell her that I couldn't get wood.
Stupid, isn't it? We'd been married for twenty-six
years and I couldn't admit that I couldn't get a hard-
on. It was a man thing, I guess. I'd already lost my
desk, and my staff, and my company limo. How was
I going to tell her that I'd lost my dick, too?"

Eventually, I persuaded Harry to tell Hannah what
was wrong, and why. I also explained to Hannah
that, with Harry home, she couldn't expect her daily
routine to continue exactly as it had before. She had
to recognize that he had a role to play, and that his

contribution to their day-to-day relationship had to amount to more than lifting his legs whenever she wanted to vacuum under the chair. She had to restructure her life so that they did things together— things that *he* wanted to do, as well as her. In exactly the same way, Harry had to learn to fit in, too, and realize that he wasn't just having an endless series of days off from work.

I encouraged them to be more sexual together, and more often. They had the whole day together, why not take advantage of it? I gave Hannah instructions on getting to know Harry's penis, and learning to fondle it. It was no longer something that stayed curled up in his business pants all day, and occasionally peeked out at night. It was his masculine identity, his totem pole. It showed that he found her sexually attractive, and she could enjoy it any time she wanted to. For his part, Harry needed to be more complimentary, more loving, more attentive, more *lustful*. He needed to remind himself why he had first found Hannah sexually exciting, and he needed to show her that he *still* found her sexually exciting.

More than anything else, they needed to learn to *talk* to each other, especially about sex and the way they felt about each other. When a man is working away from home all day, years can go by with hardly any conversation at all, apart from "How was your day?" That was another reason why Harry found it so hard to tell Hannah that he couldn't get an erection. He had never discussed anything intimate with her and he simply didn't know how. Once they had talked it over, however, both of them said that "it wasn't such a big deal, was it? And it was such a *relief*."

Of course Harry's heavy drinking had made his erectile dysfunction much worse, but once his problem was out in the open he promised to cut down on alcohol. He also promised to go to the doctor for a checkup, just to make sure that there was no physical cause for his failure to get an erection.

As it turned out, there wasn't, apart from the normal symptoms of ageing, such as a slight hardening of the arteries (atherosclerosis). But it still took him some time to regain his erections. "I get wood, and it lasts for a while, but then I start thinking about it, and I lose it."

He was "spectatoring"—detaching himself from his lovemaking as if he were an outside observer, and losing his involvement (and thus his erection).

I urged Hannah to persist with her frequent fondling to get him erect, but to make sure that once he was inside her she went through the Thirteen Steps so that he felt no pressure on him to reach a climax. The first two or three nights they did little more than Step One, which was nothing more than twenty minutes or so of "vaginal containment," with muscle squeezing but no thrusting. "It was wonderful," said Hannah. "He kept hard the whole time . . . and in fact he felt bigger than he ever had before. I told him that. I told him, 'Harry, your cock is just gigantic.' He didn't say anything, but I think I felt it grow an inch more!"

Don't think that it's only middle-aged men who suffer from psychogenic impotence. Of all the cases of ED reported amongst younger men under 35, over 70 percent had psychogenic causes. Younger men suffer from a whole variety of pressures and problems which can lead to erection failure. One young science student from Rockford, Illinois, told me that he kept losing his erection in the middle of having sex because he couldn't stop himself from visualizing his naked sister. When he was 14 he regularly used to spy on his sister through her bedroom window when she was undressing, and masturbate. Now, whenever he began to feel that his climax was approaching, he became overwhelmed with guilt and embarrassment and his erection died away.

In a case like this, it was important for him to forgive himself for what he had done when he was younger. Lots of adolescent boys spy on their older sisters, and it doesn't amount to anything more than innocent curiosity. At least he didn't charge his friends to come and spy on her, too.

Todd, a 24-year-old graphic designer from Newark, New Jersey, had such chronic erection difficulties that he stopped dating girls altogether. "What's the use? I know that if I take them to bed, nothing's going to happen." As a consequence, he was lonely and thoroughly miserable, and felt that he was never going to find a sexual partner, let alone a lifetime companion or a wife.

There was nothing *physically* wrong with Todd. He regularly bought pornographic DVDs and magazines, which gave him an erection, and he was able to masturbate to a climax. But it turned out that when he was younger, he had been skinnier and spottier than he was now, and that he was generally regarded as a "geek."

At school, he had found it very difficult to date girls, and he had never been able to attract the really pretty ones. "I didn't realize as I was growing older that I was getting better-looking. You know, the spots disappeared, and I put on some weight, and I started to dress more casual, but I still didn't have any confidence with girls."

One night in summer he went to a friend's party. "I didn't expect to score. I mean, *me,* I never scored. I always stayed in the kitchen with the other geeks, talking about *Star Wars*, and getting drunk. But I went outside to get some air and there was this girl that I knew from high school, Angela. She was blonde and very pretty, and she had huge breasts that I always used to have fantasies about. She said 'Hi' and I said 'Hi' and we got talking, and because I was drunk I had all the confidence in the world. And she *liked* me. She really liked me. She was probably slightly drunk as well, but I felt like all of my high-school geekiness had gone forever, I was a man now, and I could pick up any woman I wanted.

"I asked her to dance. Outside, in the yard, under the moon. They were playing some song by Fountains of Wayne. I kissed her and she kissed me back and the next thing I knew she was breathing in my ear that we should go upstairs. I couldn't believe it. Talk about dreams come true.

"We found a spare bedroom. The bed was all heaped up with stuffed animals like bears and rabbits and we fell on top of them and scattered them everywhere. I kissed her and I took off her top, and there they were, in the flesh, those actual breasts that I had fantasized about so often, in a white lacy bra. I fumbled around with her bra and I couldn't unhook it. She laughed at me and said I must be pretty inexperienced. I laughed it off and said, 'Inexperienced? Me? No way . . . I'm just drunk.' But I guess that dented my confidence some.

"She took off her bra herself. Her breasts were big and warm and heavy and she had these really enormous nipples. My cock was so hard by then that it was practically bursting out of my pants. I kissed her and fondled her breasts and sucked her nipples and I was in heaven, man. She squeezed my cock through my pants and said 'Come on, let's get it on.'

"I managed to pull down the zipper of her skirt and take it off her. Underneath she was wearing these tiny white lace panties to match her bra. She was being pretty aggressive, and she unbuckled my belt and pulled down my pants and my shorts. She took hold of my cock and rubbed it, and I thought 'This is it, this is amazing, this is where your whole life changes.' Her panties were see-through and I could see that she didn't have any pussy hair, which totally blew me away. Just a pink slit, peeping at me through the lace.

"It was then that she asked me to put on a condom, because she wasn't on the pill. I told her I didn't have a condom. She sat up and looked at me like I had just arrived from Mars or something. She said, 'This is a *party*. How can you not have a condom?' What was I going to say? 'I never usually score when I go to parties. I spend all evening in the kitchen talking about *Star Wars* and you don't need a condom for that.'

"My erection just died on me. I said, 'I'll get a condom. Hold on. I'll get a condom.' But I felt like a total amateur, you know? I felt like a geek again. I put my pants back on and I went downstairs and I asked my friend Lenny if he had a condom, but he didn't have a condom, either, and he started asking around, and pretty soon everybody was chanting, 'Todd needs a condom, Todd needs a condom,' and then they started asking who I needed it for, and I was so humiliated.

"Somebody gave me one, and I went back upstairs. But Angela said she wasn't in the mood any more, and she started to put her bra back on. I said, 'Come on, come on, everything's going to be great,' and I persuaded her to lie back down on the bed. I took off my pants but my cock was only half hard. I opened the condom and it turned out to be green, bright green. Angela said, 'That looks disgusting.' I tried to put on the condom but my cock went completely soft. I tried rubbing it but I felt as if I was kneeling in front of her, jerking myself off, which I *was*, I guess. That was it. All of my confidence went out of the window. I couldn't get my cock back up for anything. Angela got dressed and flounced out of the bedroom, and everybody at the party *knew* that I hadn't been able to do it."

Todd's experience is not uncommon. Most young men have humiliating sexual encounters at one time or another, and ultimately the only answer is to chalk them up to experience. But Todd was suffering from "fear of failure," and he needed to find a way of restoring his sexual confidence. He needed to be reassured that he was quite capable of achieving and keeping an erection (which he was) and of satisfying a woman in bed (which he could).

Like most men who suffer from persistent ED, Todd needed to talk to his doctor. I know that very few men like to consult their doctor about anything personal, let alone erection failure, but a doctor is the only person who can objectively assess a man's erection problem and give him the appropriate treatment.

These days, most impotence treatments are so easy and so effective that men who have procrastinated in seeking help usually end up kicking themselves that they didn't go to their doctor earlier. If your lover has trouble getting his penis to rise (or to stay hard once it's risen) he needs to see his doctor ASAP, with your help, and with your encouragement, and with your loving support. You have seen from this book how much you can do to give your lover an erection, and sustain it, but if he is going to conquer his problem once and for all, he must ask for professional help.

What will happen when he goes to talk to his doctor?

His doctor will ask him a number of questions about his sex life. He should try to answer them as frankly and completely as he can. There is no shame in erectile dysfunction, and it doesn't mean in any way that your lover is "less of a man." Quite the opposite. ED is so common that a man who has erection problems could be described as a "typical man."

These are the kinds of questions that his doctor will probably ask him.

1) Describe what happens when you try to have sex.

Your lover's answer to this question will give the doctor clues to what is causing his erection problems. There are many different causes of ED— psychological or physical or drug- or alcohol-related—and usually these factors are interlinked in ways that can be very complex and difficult to sort out. Is his drinking causing his impotence or is his impotence driving him to drink? Is he depressed because he can't sustain an erection or is the fact that he can't sustain his erection making him depressed? Your lover may admit to the doctor, for example, that he doesn't feel very aroused these days. This doesn't mean for a moment that he doesn't love you any more, or that he doesn't think you're the sexiest woman on God's earth, but it *could* indicate that he is suffering from a reduced sex drive.

2) Did your erection problems start suddenly, or did they creep up on you?

Except in cases of surgery or accident, erection problems which start *suddenly* are likely to be psychogenic. In other words, they're caused by a specific change in circumstances which is affecting your lover's life—and maybe yours, too. Erection problems which have started gradually are more likely to be related to illness or good old ageing.

3) How long have you had erection problems?

On the whole, only men who have had persistent trouble in getting an erection will need a course of medical treatment.

4) Does your partner know that you've come to get help with your erection problem?

No man should ever have to suffer erection difficulties without help and understanding from the woman in his life. It doesn't matter what the reasons for his ED are. So he doesn't seem to think that you're sexy any more, or he's drinking too much, or taking too many drugs, or he's worried about his ex-wife and visiting his children, or he thinks he's going to lose his job? Erection problems can never be solved by trying to apportion blame, and you will probably find that once his erection problems have been solved, none of the other problems seem so bad. If you can go along with your lover when he visits his doctor, so that you can all discuss his erection difficulties together, that would be very helpful. You may find that you can solve his problem on the spot. On the other hand, he may prefer to see what treatment the doctor can offer him, and whether it works, before asking you to get involved. But even if he'd rather go alone, talk about it together before he goes. Incidentally, doctors are just as willing to help single men who *don't* have partners, like Todd.

5) Why do you think you can't get an erection?

Sometimes a man will have a sneaking suspicion about why he's having erection problems, but hasn't wanted to admit it. It can help a doctor to make a diagnosis if your lover can run through anything that may have affected his life recently, such as minor illnesses, or the use (or misuse) of prescription drugs, or any possible cause of anxiety. If you accompany your lover to the doctor, and find out what's *really* been worrying him, you may be able to reassure him then and there that it doesn't matter a damn, and that you can get through it together. Janet, for example, a 34-year-old bank teller from Lewiston, Maine, wrote to tell me that when she went to the doctor with her 37-year-old partner Ted, he confessed that he had remortgaged their house without telling her because his business was going so badly. Because of this, he felt as if he had betrayed her, and hadn't taken care of her and protected her, as a man ought to. Ted required no other treatment than a reassurance from Janet that so long as he was healthy and happy and they were still together, she didn't care about money.

6) **What did you expect to gain from coming to talk to me today?**

Once your lover has plucked up the courage to consult a doctor about his erection problems, he may very well find that *talking* about it is enough to cure it. The relief of discovering that he is not alone, and that he is not suffering from anything unusual or strange, can give him back all the sexual confidence he needs. David, a 41-year-old architect from Grand Rapids, Michigan, said, "I was sitting in my doctor's consulting room, holding Kathleen's hand, and as soon as I started talking about my erection problem, and the doctor started nodding and saying 'Yes, I see, yes, I understand,' I started to get an erection. I got a hard-on, right in the middle of talking about not being able to get a hard-on! I can't tell you how relieved I felt. It was like one of those Disney cartoons when the storm clouds clear away and the sun starts shining and the birds start singing. I would say to any man with erection problems: go talk to your doctor. Today. Now. Even if you don't get a boner while you're telling him about it, at least you'll have taken the first step to getting your manhood back." To be realistic, it's not always this easy, and I can't guarantee that you're going to hear birds twittering, not right away. Sometimes a man's erection problems can be caused by a troubled relationship with his partner, and if this is the case, he might need to seek further help from experienced counselors. Or his impotence might be caused by an underlying medical condition—in which case he might need tablets or injections or other erection aids.

7) **Are you suffering from ejaculation problems? Do you ejaculate too quickly? Or does it take you too long to ejaculate? Or maybe you can't ejaculate at all?**

Unless you and your lover openly acknowledge any ejaculation problem, and discuss it between you, and deal with it, it could seriously blight your

sexual relationship. Ejaculation problems can lead
indirectly to impotence, too. We have already seen
how the "squeeze technique" and Tantric self-
discipline can hold back a man who climaxes too
soon. Some men, however, have trouble in ejaculating at all. This is sometimes because they have
guilt problems, or because they are mistrustful of
committing themselves sexually. In the case of
older men, they might need further stimulation.
The best way to deal with delayed ejaculation is
to masturbate your partner by hand so that he
shoots his sperm all over your vulva. Next time,
when he is right on the brink of his climax, insert
his penis into your vagina so that he ejaculates
inside you. He should soon lose his inhibitions
and climax normally when he makes love to you.

When your lover visits his doctor, he will be asked
to undergo a physical examination, to check if his
erection problems are being caused by any kind of
medical condition. The doctor will want to look at
his genitals, to make sure that he isn't suffering from
any swelling or infection, and that his penis is normal. As we have seen earlier, many men believe that
their penis is too small, and this can sometimes lead
to their having erectile difficulties. I talked to my
own doctor about genital examination, and he said
that in thirty years of general medical practice, he
had never seen a penis that was too small for a man
to have satisfactory sex—although plenty of men had
asked him worriedly if their penises were big
enough.

Occasionally, a man's ability to have sex might be affected by a painful bend in his penis known as Peyronie's disease. This is most common among men between the ages of 50 and 60, and it is caused by the development of a hard lump of plaque in the shaft of the penis. Not only does the sufferer feel extreme pain in his penis—so much so that he doesn't feel like intercourse—but his penis may bend so sharply that he is physically unable to insert it into his partner's vagina.

When men first contract Peyronie's disease they are often frightened that they have contracted cancer, because of the lump, but cancer within the shaft of the penis is comparatively rare. The bend in the penis grows more extreme over four to twelve weeks. Usually, it is upward, but occasionally it may be to the left or right. It is more obvious when the penis is erect.

If your lover suspects that he has Peyronie's disease, he should of course go to his doctor immediately. Unfortunately there is no cure for it, apart from self-treatment with vitamin E, which may slow it down or even halt it altogether. For your part, you should try to understand that your partner may be suffering extreme pain in his penis. The bend in his penis may make sex in your accustomed positions uncomfortable, but you should be able to find a new position which makes it easier.

The pain from Peyronie's disease usually lasts only a few months, and can be dealt with by painkillers such as paracetamol. The disease itself is self-limiting and shouldn't last longer than eighteen months to two years, after which it will stabilize.

Unfortunately the bend in your lover's penis will remain, and he may continue to suffer from erection problems, although he will still be able to father children.

A word of warning: like penis enlargement, there are dozens of wonderful treatments offered for Peyronie's disease on the Internet. If your lover has Peyronie's and is tempted by any of them, he should discuss it with his doctor first. As a general rule, the more extravagant the claims for a cure, the less likely it is to be any damn good.

Your lover's doctor will check him for diabetes, which is a common cause of erectile dysfunction. Put simply, this means that he has too much sugar in his blood. He will also test him for hormone deficiency, which will require a blood sample. If his testosterone levels are low, this may account for his lack of interest in sex.

Another test will involve an injection into your lover's penis of the drug alprostadil, which is one of a number of treatments for erection problems. This can show his doctor that he has a healthy blood supply flowing into his penis, and it can also show *him* that he is still capable of getting a very firm erection. Some men are so delighted with the hard-on which this test gives them that their sexual confidence returns as if by magic, and they don't need any more treatment.

Your lover may have to go to a hospital for further tests—in particular for hardened arteries (atherosclerosis), multiple sclerosis, or kidney disease. He shouldn't worry about this. The tests are routine, but his general practitioner won't have the facilities to carry them out.

So what happens if his doctor decides that your lover needs treatment?

The kind of treatment that he will be offered will depend very much on what has been causing his erection problems. If his problem is largely in his mind, it is likely that his doctor will suggest **psychosexual therapy,** involving both you and him.

There are two main approaches to psychosexual therapy. One is **sensate focus**, in which a couple go back to square one in their sexual relationship, and get to know each other physically all over again. Two or three times a week they stroke and caress and undress each other, but to begin with they are not allowed to have intercourse or even to touch each other's genitals.

The idea of this is to reawaken their sexual interest in each other, but without the man feeling anxious about failing to get a sustained erection.

Over a period of weeks, the caressing becomes more intimate, and the couple is allowed to stimulate each other's genitals, but they are still not permitted to have intercourse. Eventually they reach a third stage, which in some ways is similar to the first of my Thirteen Steps. Once the man has achieved an erection, he inserts it into his partner's vagina, but neither of them is allowed to move. Most men with ED tend to lose their erection almost as soon as they have penetrated their partners, so this stage is critical. If the man can keep up his erection for several minutes while he is inside his partner's vagina, then he is well on the way to overcoming his problem for good.

Another approach is **cognitive therapy**, in which a man is assisted by his therapist to identify the fears and anxieties which may be interfering with his ability to get an erection, and face up to them.

Psychosexual treatment can be very constructive, and can help both your lover and you, too. It can improve not only your physical closeness, but your ability to talk to each other about intimate matters, which many couples can't, even after years and years of living together.

While I was preparing this book I was contacted by a couple from White Plains, New York—John, 43, and Olivia, 41. They had been married for twelve years and in their own words had enjoyed "a really healthy sex life." But one of their sons died in an auto accident and soon afterward John's business had to go into Chapter 11, and as a consequence John began to suffer from erection problems. Olivia said, "We want to talk about it, but somehow we can never find the words."

For over twenty-five years I have recommended that couples spend some time early in their sexual relationships touching and describing their partner's genitals, and getting comfortable with the idea of using words like "cock" and "pussy" to each other, or any other pet words which they may prefer instead.

Olivia said, "John lay next to me and said, 'I love the color of your cunt lips . . . look at them, they're pale pink, like rose petals. And I like to stick the tip of my tongue in your pee-hole, and slide my finger into your cunt . . . it comes out all shiny and juicy.' I did the same for him, telling him how his cock was so swelled up that it looked as if it was going to burst, and how exciting it was when his balls tightened up. We had never used words like that before, but after that we made a point of using them all the time, and it wasn't very long before we could talk about our 'bits' without feeling uncomfortable. If I had a touch of thrush I could tell John that my cunt was a little bit sore, and he could say things like, 'I'm going to fill your cunt full of come,' and it was *exciting*, not embarrassing. A couple who live together and sleep together should be able to say what they like to each other, too—anything."

The disadvantages of psychosexual treatment are that it can be very expensive and time-consuming and slow. It can take months or even years for a man to overcome his erection problems through therapy. In cognitive therapy, there is also a risk that his therapist may dig up issues which he finds painful or upsetting, and which can actually make his impotence worse.

There is a wide variety of **physical treatments** for impotence, some of which are immediate and highly effective. They vary from pills to injections in the penis to vacuum pumps. Which treatment your lover chooses will depend largely on his own preference and his doctor's advice. It is worth bearing in mind, though, that physical treatments are nothing more than a chemical or a mechanical way of getting an

erection. No physical treatment can act as an aphrodisiac, or increase your partner's sex drive.

If your lover is passionate about you, a physical
treatment for impotence will help him to express that
passion because his penis will be hard. It will give
him confidence and ease some of his doubts about his
manhood, and it will probably make him a happier
person. But it won't magically solve any emotional issues that you might have in your relationship, and
it won't necessarily solve the problems that caused
his impotence in the first place. So you still have to
work at the penis fondling, and the all-night sex sessions, and more than anything else you will have to
work at developing your physical intimacy and your
spiritual togetherness. Remember, really great sex is
all about unifying your minds as well as your bodies.

Let's take a look at some of the main treatments
for impotence.

Viagra. The launch of Viagra helped enormously
to bring the subject of male erectile dysfunction to
public attention, and to make it an acceptable topic
for discussion—particularly when several ageing celebrities gave it their enthusiastic and unembarrassed
endorsement, notably Hugh Hefner, the publisher of
Playboy. Viagra was developed by Pfizer as a treatment for heart disease, but researchers soon found
that it had an interesting side effect! It is a blue,
diamond-shaped oral tablet which is sold in three
dosage strengths—25 mg, 50 mg and 100 mg. Your
lover's doctor will select the initial dose, but most
men seem to be happiest with 50 mg. Taking more
than 100 mg, which is the maximum recommended

dose, doesn't make a man any harder for any longer, but it may exacerbate the side effects (headache, stuffy nose and stomach upset).

Viagra should be swallowed whole with a glass of water about twenty minutes to an hour before anticipated sex. It will take longer to work if taken on top of a heavy meal, and its effect may very well be compromised by large quantities of alcohol. It will not give a man an erection unless he is sexually stimulated. If a man *doesn't* suffer from erection problems, Viagra won't turn him into a sex machine, although it may make him rather red in the face. No man should take it at all if it hasn't been prescribed for him by a doctor, although it is widely available on the Internet. There are a great many Viagra fakes on the market, as well as blue and purple pills with names like "V-Sex" which have absolutely no effect on erection problems.

Viagra lasts for about four to six hours, although I have had reports of its lasting for longer. It shouldn't be taken more than once a day, and it shouldn't be taken with any other medicines, especially nitrates. Nitrates are prescribed for the treatment of angina, or chest pain. Taken together with Viagra, they could dangerously lower a man's blood pressure. Men with heart or liver problems should avoid taking Viagra, too, as should men with stomach ulcers.

You shouldn't take Viagra yourself, since it is not an aphrodisiac and has not been tested for safety on women.

The main criticism of Viagra from a user's point of view is that it takes so long to work, and doesn't offer complete sexual spontaneity. Several men have complained that they have had to prolong foreplay "while waiting for the Viagra to kick in"—which may not necessarily be a bad thing for women, but which can be frustrating in a situation of urgent lust. No *9½ Weeks* antics in the elevator.

All the same, Viagra was a tremendous breakthrough in the treatment of erectile dysfunction, and the fact that it sells in its billions every year is testimony to the rediscovered sexual pleasure that it has brought to men and women of all ages all over the world. I have talked to men in their seventies and eighties who never thought that they would have sex with their wives or partners ever again, but who are regularly making love three and four times a week. It shows in their general health, in their positive attitude to life, and the spring in their step.

Cialis. Cialis is a yellow, almond-shaped tablet which works in the same way as Viagra, by relaxing the blood vessels in the penis and causing an erection. Like Viagra, Cialis is not an aphrodisiac and a man needs to be sexually stimulated in order to get hard.

The great advantage of Cialis over Viagra is that its effects last very much longer, as much as twenty-four hours, so it allows a man to be much more spontaneous in his sexual activity. It comes in two doses, 10 mg and 20 mg, with a recommended starting dose of 10 mg. It should be swallowed about a half hour before any anticipated sexual activity, with water. Food doesn't interfere with the effectiveness of Cialis, and neither does a sensible amount of alcohol.

The same restrictions apply to Cialis as they do to Viagra. Your lover shouldn't take it if he has a history of serious heart problems, or if he's taking any medicines that contain nitrates.

What is it actually *like*, taking Viagra or Cialis? I talked to dozens of men who have taken one or the other, and they all said that they felt no unusual effects whatsoever—"except that when I started to kiss my partner, and touch her breasts, my cock went hard and stayed hard, and I actually had normal sex for the first time in over a year."

Apparently some men have reported a temporary blue-colored tinge to their vision, but none of the men I spoke to had experienced it.

Uprima. This is the brand name for apomorphine hydrochloride, which works in a different way altogether than Viagra and Cialis. It is a light brown tablet which comes in two doses—2 mg (pentagon-shaped) and 3 mg (triangular). A man places the tablet under his tongue and allows it to dissolve, so that its contents are absorbed into his bloodstream. It takes about ten minutes to dissolve, and about ten to twenty minutes before it starts to work.

Like Viagra and Cialis, Uprima will only give a man an erection if he is sexually stimulated. But unlike Viagra and Cialis, it works by targeting a specific area in the brain known to trigger erections, and it enhances the signals which allow a man's penis to rise. Because Uprima is dissolved under the tongue, its effectiveness is not impaired by food or moderate amounts of alcohol.

Men who are taking medicines containing nitrates should not take Uprima; neither should men who have uncontrolled high or low blood pressure, or who are suffering from serious heart conditions.

Uprima can make a man dizzy and light-headed, so the manufacturers advise that he shouldn't drive for at least two hours after taking it. You've got it . . . that means you'll have to invite him to stay the night.

Injection therapy. If a man injects certain drugs into his penis, it relaxes the blood vessels so that blood flows freely into his corpora cavernosa and gives him an erection. These days, the most commonly used drug is a prostaglandin known as alprostadil. It is identical to a prostaglandin that naturally occurs in the penis and is involved in the natural erection process. It can give a man an erection within ten minutes, and generally keep him erect for about an hour.

Injection therapy has a very high rate of success—even higher than oral tablets—and many men who have suffered from long-term erection problems say that they are "very satisfied" with their sex lives as a result. An impressive proportion of men have reported that after a course of injection therapy they have regained the ability to get spontaneous erections.

If your lover wants to try injection therapy he will need a steady hand and good eyesight since the drug has to be injected right into the body of his penis. It would be an advantage, too, if he didn't suffer from "needle phobia." The needles used to inject alprostadil are very fine and a man will suffer only a tiny prick (although this is not a phrase I recommend you use to any man who has doubts about the size of his penis).

Some men say that their penis aches after injection, but this is likely to be the effect of the drug rather than the injection itself. Occasionally an alprostadil erection can last too long—from four to six hours—which may require medical intervention. There is also a possibility that the tissues within the penis may harden over a period of time (fibrosis), although this hardening is usually reversed if treatment is stopped.

MUSE. It might sound poetic, but MUSE is an acronym for Medicated Urethral System for Erection. MUSE was developed in the United States after it was discovered that a man's urethra can absorb certain medications, which can then filter into the surrounding tissue of his penis, and cause an erection.

The medication used in MUSE is alprostadil—the same prostaglandin used in injection therapy. It comes in three dosages—250 mg, 500 mg and 1000 mg. A pellet of alprostadil is supplied in a specially designed plastic applicator. The applicator has a narrow stem which can be inserted into the urethra. The user then pushes a button at the top, and the pellet is released.

The makers of MUSE recommend that a man urinate immediately prior to injecting the prostaglandin pellet, because this lubricates his urethra and makes it easier for the pellet to go down. MUSE is mainly for men who don't like the idea of injecting their penis with a hypodermic, although it isn't nearly as effective. Only about 30–40 percent of ED sufferers find it suitable, and very few of them find that the lowest dosage gives them a long-lasting erection.

The most common side effect of MUSE is mild penis pain. This is caused not only by pushing a pellet into the urethra, but by the comparatively high dosage of alprostadil required to get the same effect as an injection. On the plus side, nobody has yet complained of a six-hour erection that has to be taken to the emergency room.

In their excellent book, *Impotence*, published by the Royal Society of Medicine in Britain, Philip Kell and Wallace Dinsmore remark that the principal disadvantage of MUSE as far as they can see is the manual dexterity required—"especially in obese patients who are unable to see their penis except in the bathroom mirror!"

Vacuum pumps. We have comprehensively covered the subject of vacuum pumps in our earlier chapter on penis enlargement, but pumps are also commonly used to help men with ED to get an erection. Your partner will fit a rubber constrictor ring around the base of his penis, and then insert his penis into the cylinder of a battery-operated vacuum pump.

When he switches on the pump, some of the air will be evacuated out of the cylinder and blood will flow into his penis to give him an erection ("Nature abhors a vacuum," as we all learned in science class). When his penis is hard, he takes it out of the pump, but keeps the constrictor ring in place to prevent the blood from flowing out of his penis and back into his body.

Vacuum pumps are simple to use and have no side effects (apart from bruising and blistering if they are overused for the purposes of penis enlargement). Unfortunately they are far from spontaneous, and some women complain that they make their partner's penis feel a little chilly.

Some men with erection difficulties have asked me if the male hormone testosterone would help them. A course of testosterone might increase a man's sexual desire, but it has no effect on his ability to get an erection. In fact, it will probably compound his problems by making him feel even more frustrated and useless.

I have also been asked about yohimbine. This is a drug made from the bark of the *Pausinystalin yohimbe* tree, and the story goes that a missionary in Africa was shocked to find it being used by a local tribe as an aphrodisiac. A limited study showed that in cases of psychogenic impotence, 31 percent of men who took yohimbine reported an improvement in their ability to get an erection, compared to 5 percent who were given a placebo (a pill with no chemical effect, used for research purposes). In a trial on men suffering from organic impotence, yohimbine had no effect, but study is continuing, and the African aphrodisiac may one day prove to be a valuable aid to erections.

Surgical treatment. If all other treatments fail, your partner might consider having a prosthetic implant in his penis to assist him in getting an erection. This is a drastic step, but it can help men who have seriously diseased veins or arteries, or hardening of the tissue in the body of the penis (fibrosis).

In surgical treatment, two parallel plastic rods are inserted into the corpora cavernosa of the penis. Depending on his personal preference and medical advice, your partner can choose from:

Semirigid rod prostheses. These are two rods which contain braided wires or hinges which can be manually bent to give your partner an erection.

Inflatable penis prostheses (self-contained). These are two rods similar in appearance to the semirigid rods, but containing saline solution which is pumped from a reservoir at one end to give them rigidity. They are deflated after sex by operating a release valve.

Two-piece inflatable prostheses. The rods for this device are attached by tubes to a pump reservoir the size and shape of a testicle, containing saline solution. The pump reservoir is surgically inserted into the scrotum, and whenever your partner wants an erection, he simply squeezes his balls. The advantage of two-piece prostheses over self-contained prostheses is that they can hold more saline solution, and thus give greater rigidity. Because of the size of the pump reservoir, however, your partner may not be able to go totally flaccid when he is not having sex.

Three-piece inflatable prostheses. These are the Cadillacs of penis implants. Two inflatable cylinders are inserted into the corpora cavernosa of the penis, and these are connected to a small pump device inserted into the scrotum, next to the testicles. This in turn is connected to a reservoir of saline solution placed inside the abdomen. Three-piece inflatable prostheses can carry even more saline solution than two-piece prostheses, which means that they can usually give your partner a much more satisfactory hard-on—bigger, thicker and longer. But they can also empty more completely, so that when he isn't making love his penis returns to being soft and squidgy like that of any other man. In surgeon-speak, "His carriage under his clothing will be more acceptable." In other words, his dick won't stick out.

Studies have shown that men with inflatable penis implants are usually very satisfied—and their partners are, too. There can of course be complications, as with any surgical procedure, but your partner's doctor will be able to advise him of the risks.

In only a few years, the treatments available to men with ED have improved beyond belief. Unlike treatments for other conditions, there is such a wide variety that a man who finds that one kind of treatment doesn't work can always try another, and another, and another. Big business is taking erectile dysfunction very seriously (as well as the potential profits of treating it). Wm. Wrigley Jr. Co., the makers of Juicy Fruit, Big Red and Doublemint, have been granted a U.S. patent to develop chewing gum containing sildenafil, the chemical name for Viagra. Wrigley researchers say that the gum would provide "an improved dosage form and method of treating erectile dysfunction." It would be easier on the stomach than Viagra pills, and would work faster.

The most effective treatment for ED, however, is *you*. I can't emphasize too strongly that if your partner is suffering from erection problems, he needs (a) your understanding; and (b) your active encouragement in seeking professional help. Erectile dysfunction is nothing to be ashamed of, and it doesn't mean that a man is any less sexy.

Lena, a 37-year-old Realtor from Napa, California, told me, "When I first asked Gerry if he was having trouble getting an erection, he burst into tears. He said that he loved me just as much as ever, and that he wanted to make love to me, but for some reason that he couldn't understand, his cock just wouldn't get hard. I told him to dry his eyes and not to worry about it. If there was something wrong, we'd fix it, and we'd fix it together.

"I started to fondle him, the way you suggested, but I never made him feel that he had to get hard. I did a lot of oral sex, too, which I'd never done much before, and I think that was what really got him going again. I still didn't make him feel that he *had* to make love to me, but after two or three weeks I had such a good relationship with his cock that he wanted to join in, just to show me whose cock it actually was.

"We still don't know exactly why he couldn't get it on. Maybe it was stress, who knows? But it's over now, and our love life is all the better for it."

Afterword

Of all the changes that have taken place since I first started giving advice about sex and sexual relationships over thirty years ago, the most important has been the increasing willingness of men and women to discuss their personal problems openly, and to seek help when they feel that they need it.

For that, we can thank all of the so-called agony aunts who have pioneered frank sexual discussion on TV, on the radio, and in magazines. Some of their advice has been excellent, some of it has been dubious, and some of it has been downright wacky. But over the years they have given people a forum in which they can articulate their desires, their passions, their pleasures and their disappointments.

Men's sexual performance remains one of the most difficult of subjects to tackle, however, because even today most men are very reluctant to admit that they're having trouble in getting an erection. Women can find it a baffling and hurtful problem to deal with, particularly when they believe that their partner doesn't find them attractive any more. "He must have lost interest in me. Whatever I do, I can't give him a hard-on."

I hope I have been able to show you that your man's penis may belong to him, but his erection belongs to both of you. That is what makes your lovemaking pleasurable and satisfying and spiritually meaningful. Once you have read this book and put some of my suggestions into practice, I am confident that you and your lover will discover a sexual experience that—in every sense of the word—will always keep you "up."

Three: Size of Contentment

Can He Make It Bigger?

Does the size of a man's penis matter?

The straight answer to that question is that it does—and it doesn't. It depends who you're asking.

It matters very much to some men who think that they have small penises, or below-average penises, because it makes them feel sexually inferior.

On the other hand, penis size hardly matters at all to most women. A woman may certainly find the *idea* of a huge penis sexually exciting—just as a man will find the idea of 44FF breasts sexually exciting— and if an attractive man turns out to have a rather large appendage, she will count herself lucky. But if most women were asked to write down their top ten criteria for choosing a sexual partner, "huge penis" wouldn't rate very highly, if at all.

There is hardly any serious research on the subject of penis size and what women think about it, and the few statistics that *are* available are highly contradictory. But serious and not-so-serious surveys into getting to know your partner both physically and mentally, and that is why I have stressed how important it is for you to make a friend of your partner's penis. You may very well be shy about doing it at first. For his part, he may wonder what the hell you're doing, constantly trying to get into his pants. But don't give up. Do it teasingly, flirtatiously—the way you first made a friend of *him*.

Jodie, 24, a telephone salesperson from Houston, Texas, said, "Whenever my boyfriend and I sleep together, I always rest my head on his stomach after we've made love, and suck his cock like a comforter. He says it's real relaxing, and sometimes it sends us both to sleep. But other times it stiffens up again, and the next thing we know we're at it again. I can always tell if that's going to happen, even before he does, because I can feel it swelling up in my mouth. So I guess you could say that I know his cock even better than he does. Sometimes I tell him that if he doesn't behave himself, I'll dump him and go out with his cock instead."